NATIONAL
GEOGRAPHIC

POCKET GUIDE TO THE
Trees & Shrubs
OF NORTH AMERICA

NATIONAL
GEOGRAPHIC

POCKET GUIDE TO THE
Trees & Shrubs
OF NORTH AMERICA

BLAND CROWDER

NATIONAL GEOGRAPHIC
WASHINGTON, D.C.

CONTENTS

Trees & Shrubs
The Living Landscape

What differentiates a tree from a shrub? This guide deals with 160 species of trees and shrubs likely to be encountered in the United States and Canada. Defining a species as a tree or a shrub can be difficult, especially considering how variable many species are. The word is wood. Like herbaceous annuals, biennials, and perennials, trees and shrubs grow mostly at their tip, or apex, which contains the apical meristem, where the growing cells divide. But trees and shrubs also grow outward, laterally. Lateral growth occurs in lateral meristems. Growth patterns and aging result in several kinds of tissues that in concert allow these sometimes behemoth plants to arise. Woody plants include small trees, bushes, shrubs, and many vines.

Anatomy of a Tree Trunk

Let us imagine that we are looking at the stump of a just felled tree that had been evolved just so naturalists could learn the basic anatomy of wood. We are looking at a cross section of the tree, taken near its base, in which we can see perfectly its bark and other layers. Let us consider those layers, from the outside in, remembering that the same layers may be found on a smaller scale on the tree's branches, twigs, and roots. There are three main layers—the bark, the cambium, and the wood, some of them divided further.

Bark, of course, is a tree's external covering. This layer of dead corklike cells protects the interior from injury and disease and conserves water.

The inner bark, or phloem, is a transport system that moves food and other substances made during photosynthesis (usually taking place in the leaves) to the rest of the tree. As new bark is produced, it pushes older cells outward. Eventually the older bark cannot retain all this newer bark, and its smooth complexion cracks, flakes, or peels.

Between the inner bark and the wood lies the cambium, the lateral meristems, where the cells that make the tree grow wider multiply. New cells form to its outside and its inside.

Toward the center of the trunk, inside the cambium, is the wood, or xylem. Wood contains strengthening fibers and other conducting vessels. There are two kinds of wood. The sapwood, adjacent to the cambium, transports water and dissolved minerals and nutrients from the soil (taken up by roots) to the rest of the tree.

When the cambium creates new wood cells, their size and shape depend on the conditions in the area at the time, so in the generally wetter spring, new cells are bigger, and in the drier summer, they are smaller. These differences make visible annual rings (each actually representing a layer of wood), which of course are an index of a tree's age.

With time, some xylem layers closer to the center of the trunk die, no longer needed for transport. This older wood, called heartwood, fills with substances, like resins, that protect it from rot. It is often darker than the surrounding wood.

Without the development of this miraculous system, we would not have trees and shrubs. The wood varies with the kind of tree or shrub, and properties of the different parts of the trunk also vary.

A resilient dogwood blossoms under a cover of trees in a foggy forest.

People have exploited these differences for millennia, using different species in making canoes, clothing, medicines, food, shelter,
charcoal, decorations, or fire.

Guide Organization

The guide is organized in several ways. The overarching scheme
is the most major. First discussed are the gymnosperms. The word
means "naked seed," and for our purposes, it is another way of
saying conifers. The conifers include the cedars, the cypresses, the
pines, and the spruces, whose seeds are bare in the cone and not
surrounded by a fruit. (The Ginkgo, which does make fruit, and a
nasty one at that, is considered a conifer.) The other major group is
the angiosperms, whose seeds are enclosed by fruits (the mature
ovary). The angiosperms are divided into the dicots (which have two
cotyledons, or seed leaves), which include oaks, the Mountain Laurel,
birches, locusts, and the Jumping Cholla, and the monocots (which
have but one cotyledon), which include the Joshua Tree, the palms,
and the palmettos.

Principles Used in the Entries

As you use the entries, keep in mind a few principles that are followed. *General* is probably the most important trait for these descriptions. Multivolume sets have been published on wood morphology,
reproductive strategies, taxonomy, ranges, and ecology of trees and
shrubs. Detailed, torturous keys get to the nitty-gritty of identification.
All these books are available at libraries and bookstores. This guide
is meant to whet readers' interest and to truly help them identify
trees and shrubs that they may see on field trips and travels, and to
tell them something about the species' ecology, value to wildlife and
humans, and status—including whether or not they are native.

Geographic ranges are general and refer to a plant's native range.
It is not noted that conifers are evergreen, which most are; some,
however, are deciduous (the Baldcypress, for example), and this is
pointed out. Likewise, it is not stated when an angiosperm tree is
deciduous, because most of them are; but some are evergreen or
mostly so (the Wax Myrtle, for example), and this too is pointed out.

Snow dusts aspen and spruce trees in Colorado's Rocky Mountain National Park.

Though some entries mention culinary uses of various tree or shrub parts, readers should not eat any part of any plant unless they are 100 percent certain that it is 100 percent safe. Other species are described as being toxic; if a species is not so described, it should not be deduced that any part is safe to eat.

The descriptions of the trees and shrubs are designed to convey the species' unique features and those that are most helpful in identification, most important the height (following the scientific name) and the information under Key Facts; the photographs and illustrations complement each other. Features of twigs are rarely described. Floras often describe twigs, as do books that teach users to identify deciduous trees in winter. Depending on latitude, altitude, soil characteristics, or sunlight, two individuals of a species can look quite different. The species entries take into account much of the variation by a descriptive phrase, or a range of the numbers.

Trees & You

Not only will this guide help you get to know and more deeply appreciate this starter set of 160 species, it will help you see the forest in addition to the trees—and something larger than that, albeit not definable or quantifiable. The spirit of North America, and of its peoples, indigenous and not, is inseparable from these amazing woody plants.

KEY IDENTIFYING FEATURES

Conifers have four types of leaf arrangement:

❶ Fascicles are bunches of needles growing from one bud.

❷ Pectinate rows are arranged in ranks along opposite sides of the shoot.

❸ Awl-shaped leaves are set radially around the shoot.

❹ Scalelike leaves are set densely around the shoot.

Broadleaf trees have more varied foliage than the conifers. Some examples of types of foliage shape include:

❺ Pinnately lobed: many lobes radiating from the leaf's midrib

❻ Ovate: egg-shaped with broad end at the base

❼ Pinnately compound: many small leaflets arranged in pairs on either side of a central midrib

❽ Deltoid: triangular with stem attached to the middle of the base

❾ Palmately lobed: hand-shaped structure with more than three lobes branching from a single point at the base

❿ Lanceolate: general shape of a lance—longer than wide and a pointed apex

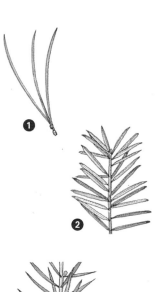

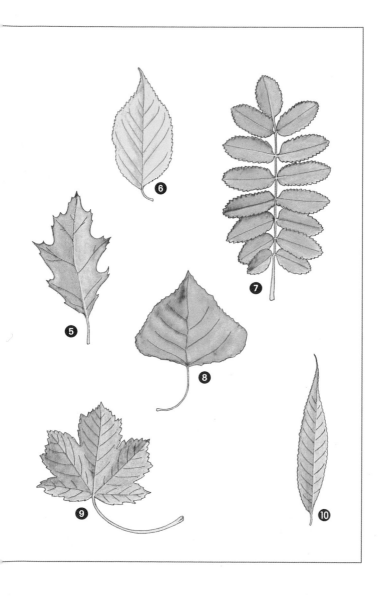

Ginkgo/Maidenhair Tree

Ginkgo biloba H to 130 ft (40 m)

The Ginkgo is considered a conifer, though it does not produce cones. It is deciduous, quickly losing its distinctive leaves after a bright yellow autumn phase.

KEY FACTS

This tree fares well in gardens and cities; *biloba* refers to its leaves, usually 2-lobed.

+ leaves: Fan-shaped, recalling maidenhair fern

+ flowers/fruits: Sexes on different trees, male in catkin-like clusters, female 1 or 2 on short stalk

+ range: Survives mainly in cultivation

Ginkgo biloba is the only species in a genus that millions of years ago had nearly worldwide distribution. The native of China is now prized around the world for its beauty and its ability to withstand pollution and other adverse conditions—including atomic bomb blasts. (A group of trees just one mile/ 1.6 km from ground zero at Hiroshima survived, regained their health, and still grow there.) The fruit mature on the female flower stalks and recall small plums—until they fall to the ground and decay, earning the tree another alias, "stink-bomb tree."

Alaska Cedar/Yellow Cypress/Nootka Cypress

Chamaecyparis nootkatensis H 49–125 ft (15–38 m)

Typical of false cypresses (often incorrectly called cedars), this species is aromatic and resinous. Cones mature in two years.

KEY FACTS

Branches droop in flat sprays.

+ leaves: Scales pressed together, bluish green; unpleasant odor

+ cones: Male and female on same tree at branchlet tips; mature seed cones of 4–6 short-pointed scales, reddish brown

+ range: Coastal mountains, southeastern Alaska to northern California

Prized for its durable, fine-grained wood, the Alaska Cedar is slow growing and long lived, so that a tree can be much older than the diameter of its trunk would suggest. One individual is 3,500 years old. The tree was important to indigenous peoples of its range, including the Nuu-chah-nulth (formerly called Nootka). It is used in landscaping in the coastal Northwest. This species was originally assigned to the genus *Cupressus* (the true cypresses), then to *Chamaecyparis,* but it may be assigned to a new genus, *Xanthocyparis,* because it is felt to differ strongly from the other two genera.

Atlantic White Cedar
Chamaecyparis thyoides H to 82 ft (25 m)

A medium to large tree reminiscent of the junipers, the Atlantic White Cedar grows in pure stands or, less often, with wet-woods trees like Baldcypress and Blackgum.

KEY FACTS

Branches are in fan-shaped sprays; bark is not shredded.

+ leaves: Scales tightly overlapping

+ cones: Male and female on same tree but separate branches; mature cones of 6 pointed, woody scales

+ range: Maine to Florida to Mississippi, mainly in swamps and wet sands of Coastal Plain

The wood of the Atlantic White Cedar is so appealing that the species has been overharvested—since the time of the American Revolution. Its stands are much reduced, though it is still commercially important in parts of its range. Its wood is light, strong, and easily worked, ideal for use in posts and telephone poles, barrels, shipbuilding, and decoy carving. Aromatic, it repels insects, retards decay, and resists disease, such as cedar-apple rust (unlike the Eastern Redcedar, for which the tree can be mistaken if not in fruit). Shade tolerant and attractive, the tree is often planted in yards and gardens.

Eastern Redcedar

Juniperus virginiana H to 100 ft (30 m)

The Eastern Redcedar is our most widespread conifer and one of the most common, found in fields, fencerows (thanks to seed dispersal by birds on fences), dry, open woods, and along roads.

KEY FACTS

Branchlets often droop.

+ **leaves:** Mature leaves scalelike, overlapping; foliage needle-like

+ **cones:** Male and female cones are mostly on separate trees; female cones mature into bluish berries.

+ **range:** East of Great Plains, from southeastern Canada to the Gulf of Mexico

The aromatic wood of this slow-growing juniper (it is not a true cedar) is perhaps best known for its use in lining cedar chests and closets; its aroma repels moths and other insects. It is also used for posts, paneling, and carving. Its reddish brown bark peels off in strips. Many cultivars have been developed for landscaping. The tree is the primary host to the fungus that causes cedar-apple rust, which produces masses of orange, gelatinous spore tubes among its needles. The fungus's secondary hosts are members of the rose family, such as pear and apple trees, where it is more damaging, affecting fruit crops.

Redwood/California Redwood
Sequoia sempervirens H to 375 ft (115 m)

The giant Redwood is locally common in protected areas along rivers experiencing extensive rainfall and constant fogs off the ocean.

KEY FACTS

The world's tallest tree, named for its thick, reddish bark, can live longer than 2,000 years.

+ **needles:** Dark green

+ **cones:** Male and female in separate clusters on same tree; seed cones oblong, red-brown

+ **range:** Pacific coast, southwestern Oregon to central California

Redwoods have limbs to a height of 50–100 feet (16–30 m), above which the trunk has many vertical stems. This unique habitat accumulates water, develops soils, and supports vertebrates, insects, and epiphytic plants. Not only is the tree's habitat characterized by fog, the tree induces fog drip, condensing water and supplying organisms in its crown and the ground below. Its wood is smooth, straight grained, and strong, with great appeal for building and woodworking. Since Spanish settlement, more than 90 percent of the largest Redwoods have been logged. The tree is now well managed.

Giant Sequoia

Sequoiadendron giganteum H 250–290 ft (76–88 m)

This massive tree was named for Sequoyah, a 19th-century Cherokee silversmith who devised a character set for writing in the tribe's language and published papers and books in Cherokee.

KEY FACTS

Columnar trunk is fluted; bark is reddish brown, as thick as 2 ft (0.6 m) at the base.

+ leaves: Scalelike, pointed, blue-green

+ cones: Egg-shaped, woody seed cones, similar to a Redwood's, but larger

+ range: Restricted to 75 groves in California, on western slopes of the Sierra Nevada

The sole surviving *Sequoiadendron* species, the Giant Sequoia includes some of the world's largest and oldest organisms. The crown can develop secondary trunks and hollow spaces, providing cover, nesting, and foraging opportunities for wildlife. The wood resists decay, but it is brittle, and harvest difficulties have also limited its commercial importance. Fire suppression threatens the Sequoia, as species naturally limited by fire can thrive in the understory. The Sequoia's thick bark can normally resist fires, but the understory trees act as fire ladders, allowing the flames to reach the giants' highly flammable crowns.

Baldcypress

Taxodium distichum H 65–130 ft (20–40 m)

A majestic, deciduous conifer of wet areas, the Baldcypress in the deeper South is commonly home to the epiphytic, grayish bromeliad Spanish moss, hanging from its limbs.

KEY FACTS

The trunk base is enlarged, fluted, and surrounded by knobby, woody "knees."

+ **leaves:** Flat, 2-ranked, feather-like, turning russet in autumn

+ **cones:** Rounded, wrinkled seed cones

+ **range:** Southeast; wet areas in Coastal Plain, inland to Texas and up the Mississippi River to Illinois and Indiana

An array of cultivars of the Baldcypress have been developed, and the tree is grown coast to coast, and it can survive in areas that are drier and decidedly less gothic than its familiar swampy habitat—including on city streets. The species' most menacing disease is "pecky cypress," a sometimes deadly brown pocket rot caused by a fungus that attacks the heartwood. Insects damage the leaves, cone, and bark. Humans, too, pose a threat, by draining wetlands and overharvesting for timber. The attractive wood is easily worked and decay resistant, used in shingles, flooring, cabinetry, trim work, beams, and barrels.

Arborvitae/Eastern White Cedar

Thuja occidentalis H to 65 ft (20 m)

The Eastern White Cedar is at home in moist or wet soil, where it outcompetes other trees. It is most populous in the Great Lakes region and farther north and is somewhat shade tolerant.

KEY FACTS

Short branches to the ground form flat sprays; reddish, shredding bark.

+ leaves: Scales sometimes long-pointed

+ cones: Male and female cones on same tree; female greenish, turning brown, with 8–12 pointed scales

+ range: Manitoba to Hudson Bay, south to Iowa and South Carolina

This native evergreen can live more than 800 years, and individuals growing in Ontario are the oldest trees in eastern North America. The Ojibwe discovered its value in construction and medicine. After they taught 16th-century French explorer Jacques Cartier to use its vitamin C–rich foliage to treat scurvy, it earned the name Arborvitae ("tree of life" in Latin). The decay-resistant, fragrant wood is used as posts and in boats, cabins, and shingles. Its oils find purpose in disinfectants and insecticides. The Eastern White Cedar is popular as an ornamental, and numerous cultivars have been developed.

Pacific Silver Fir

Abies amabilis H to 151 ft (46 m)

The Pacific Silver Fir is commonly found in moist coastal coniferous forests, to the tree line in the mountains but to sea level from Vancouver Island, British Columbia, northward.

KEY FACTS

Spire-like crown rounds with age.

+ **needles:** Attached spirally but twisted at base, lying flat on and above the stem; dark green above, silvery below

+ **cones:** Male and female on same tree; cylindrical, upright seed cones, not stalked, green, becoming purple to brown

+ **range:** Alaska to northwestern California

Soft and weak, the Pacific Silver Fir's wood is an important source of pulp used in plywood, crates, and poles. But the tree is attractive, and cultivars have been developed, though they are planted mostly in its native range and in parts of New Zealand and Scotland that can supply the requisite cool, humid summers. Indigenous peoples in its range used its sap as chewing gum, made bedding of the branches, and burned the wood. The trees are associated with hemlocks and other firs, among others, assemblages that provide food and habitat for sooty and spruce grouse, squirrels, and a bird named Clark's Nutcracker.

Balsam Fir

Abies balsamea H to 66 ft (20 m)

The Balsam Fir, whose shape is a slim pyramid, is common in moist places and swamps, as well as on well-drained hillsides. Growth is strongest and fastest in full sun.

KEY FACTS

Seed bracts extend slightly if at all beyond cone scales.

+ **needles:** Two-ranked, flattened, grooved above

+ **cones:** Erect, rounded cylinders; purple, browning with age

+ **range:** From Alberta to Labrador south to the Great Lakes and northeastern states, south to Virginia in higher mountains

The Balsam Fir is common, often dominant in its moist habitats, occurring with White Spruce, Black Spruce, Trembling Aspen, or Paper Birch. It has been heavily damaged by the Balsam Woolly Adelgid, an invasive insect introduced from Europe. The foliage and seeds provide food and cover for wildlife, including birds, squirrels, moose, and porcupines. In addition to providing pulpwood, this handsome tree is planted as an ornamental and favored as a Christmas tree. Its fragrant resin (balsam) is used in incense, rodent repellent, and to make Canada balsam, which has served as a cement for eyeglass lenses and been used to treat colds.

Fraser Fir/She-balsam

Abies fraseri H mostly to 80 ft (25 m)

The population of the Fraser Fir has been reduced as much as 95 percent by the Balsam Woolly Adelgid, an insect introduced into North America from Europe in the early 1900s.

KEY FACTS

The seed bracts protrude between cone scales.

+ needles: As in Balsam Fir, with a pine-like scent

+ cones: Male and female on same tree; seed cones purple, browning with age

+ range: Rare in high Appalachian forests of southwestern Virginia and adjacent North Carolina and Tennessee

In the wild, the Fraser Fir grows in pure stands or with other evergreens and with birches and other hardwood. It is popular as a Christmas tree, for which it is farmed, but it is intolerant of warm climate, so its culture is being reconsidered in some areas where temperatures are increasing. For better or for worse, it is sometimes called She-balsam because resin can be "milked" from its bark blisters (not true of the balsam-bearing Red Spruce, *Picea rubens,* called He-balsam). "Balsam" describes fragrant oily or resinous substances found in a number of trees and shrubs that are not necessarily close botanical relatives.

Grand Fir

Abies grandis H to 260 ft (80 m)

The majestic Grand Fir reaches its greatest size in the rain forests of Washington's Olympic Peninsula and inhabits moist forests from sea level to 4,900 feet (1,500 m).

KEY FACTS

Branches are short and drooping.

+ needles: Shorter at stem tips; 2-ranked, dark green above, 2 white bands beneath

+ cones: Seed cones barrel-shaped, upright on crown branches; seed bracts not visible

+ range: Southern British Columbia to northern California

This stately, long-lived fir is common in its range, growing in mixed coniferous and hardwood stands, often with Douglas-fir and Larch. The Grand Fir's resin has been used in wood finishing, and its wood is valuable in the paper and building industries. The tree has also been used medicinally. Commercially, it is most important in Idaho, although in general it has not proved to be a good species for landscaping outside its native range. It is an important source of food and cover for small mammals, seed-eating birds, and game birds, and it is often a host to the parasitic fir Dwarf Mistletoe.

California Red Fir
Abies magnifica H to 120 ft (37 m)

A large evergreen conifer that often dominates the montane forests of California and Oregon, the California Red Fir is distinguished by its blue-gray needles and reddish brown bark.

KEY FACTS

Short, horizontal limbs make the tree slim.

+ **needles:** Sharp, curving atop shoot; with whitish coating when young, aging to bluish green, with white bands beneath

+ **cones:** Seed cones rounded, cylindrical, borne at crown; bracts not visible beyond scales

+ **range:** Mountains of Oregon and California

At home in altitudes from 5,250 to 9,350 feet (1,600 to 2,850 m), the long-lived California Red Fir often grows in dense, pure stands, but is sometimes associated with other conifers when near the tree line. Its branches have a camphor-like aroma. As in many firs, the fatty seeds provide energy-rich food for rodents and other small mammals, and the shoots are fodder for deer. Its wood is stronger than that of other firs, and it is an important source of wood for the pulp industry and construction and as fuel and Christmas trees. The tree is plagued by heart rot and Dwarf Mistletoe.

Tamarack/Eastern Larch

Larix laricina H to 80 ft (25 m)

A slow-growing, conic, deciduous conifer, the Tamarack is heat intolerant, which explains its greatly northern distribution and why it is seldom sought in landscaping far from its native range.

KEY FACTS

Bark is scaly, pinkish to red-brown.

+ **needles:** Soft, 3-sided, in tufts on spurs, turning yellow before falling

+ **cones:** Male and female in separate clusters on same plant; seed cones upright, unstalked, egg-shaped, persisting

+ **range:** All Canadian provinces, Great Lakes and northeastern states

A common tree of swampy forests and moist uplands in its boreal zone, the Tamarack is one of our most northerly trees and has a large natural range. It grows in pure stands or is found in conjunction with Balsam Firs and other conifers. Browsed but not seriously harmed by deer, a tree can fall victim to porcupines that girdle it while feeding on its bark. The larch sawfly can damage or even kill Tamaracks by defoliating them. The wood is hard and resinous and provides lumber used for railroad ties, construction, poles, and pulp. Wild animals use its seeds.

|||||||||||||||||||||||||||||||||||||||||||||||||||||||||||||||||||||||||||||||||||||||

White Spruce

Picea glauca H to 131 ft (40 m)

Our northernmost tree, the White Spruce is widespread in bogs, on bodies of water, and on rocky hills, often found with such trees as Balsam Fir, Eastern Hemlock, and Red Maple.

KEY FACTS

This species is dense, with a conical crown, becoming cylindrical.

+ needles: Four-sided, individual, on peg-like stalk

+ cones: Unisexual, on same tree; seed cones pendulous, slender, maturing to brown; scales flexible

+ range: Alaska through all Canadian provinces to Great Lakes states and New England

The White Spruce is valued in Canada for lumber and paper pulp, and it is popular for Christmas trees, landscaping, and as a windbreak. Its needles are aromatic—but they are not exactly mountain fresh and have earned it the labels "skunk spruce" and "cat spruce." *Picea* is Latin for "pitch," a reference to resins in the bark. Spruce Beetles have destroyed 2.3 million acres in Alaska; it is susceptible to Spruce Budworm and Spruce Sawfly, and rusts make it shed its needles early. South Dakota's state tree is a variety known as the Black Hills Spruce *(P. glauca* var. *densata),* but not all authorities recognize the variety.

Black Spruce

Picea mariana H to 98 ft (30 m)

A widely distributed, small, slow-growing conifer of the continent's coldest regions, the Black Spruce inhabits moist flatlands and lake margins and, in its southern extent, sphagnum bogs.

KEY FACTS

This spruce is spire-like; its branches droop with ends upturned.

+ needles: Four-sided, blue-green above, paler, powdery below

+ cones: Unisexual, on same tree; seed cones clustered in crown

+ range: Alaska through all Canadian provinces to Great Lakes states and New England

In addition to reproducing by seeds, the Black Spruce can propagate asexually; the lower limbs can touch the ground, often under the weight of snow, and sometimes take root, creating a circle of smaller trees around the main trunk of the parent. The tree is similar to the Red Spruce but is usually found in more extreme conditions and is more northern. Its form varies; for example, at the tree line, it is often prostrate. Because the tree is small, the wood is useful for little more than pulp and fuel. It is of low value for wildlife food but provides cover for small mammals and important nesting habitat for birds.

Blue Spruce/Colorado Spruce

Picea pungens H 65–82 ft (20–25 m)

The slow-growing Blue Spruce is a medium-size evergreen probably best known from its widespread planting in Canada, the U.S., and Europe. At least 38 cultivars have been developed.

KEY FACTS

In aging, this spruce becomes more layered.

+ needles: Bluish green, sharp, 4-sided, on all sides of stem

+ cones: Unisexual, on same tree; seed cones slender, cylindrical, hanging from upper branches

+ range: High in Rocky Mountains from Idaho and Wyoming across Utah and Colorado to Arizona and New Mexico

The Blue Spruce has been called the "most beautiful species of conifer" for its stately form and "vibrant" blue to silvery hue (though this is more common in cultivars than in natural trees). Its primary value is in its looks, which horticulturists have exploited. It usually has a sporadic distribution or is a component of mixed-conifer forests, with Douglas-fir, Engelmann Spruce, and others. Not a favorite forage for wildlife, it does provide seeds for birds and cover for deer. It is plagued by the Spruce Bark Beetle, Spruce Gall Aphid, Spruce Budworm, and Spruce Spider Mite.

Engelmann Spruce

Picea engelmannii H to 164 ft (50 m)

With the Subalpine Fir *(Abies lasiocarpa),* Engelmann Spruce forms one of the most frequent forest types in the Rocky Mountains. At high elevations, it is one of the largest trees.

KEY FACTS

A spire-like tree, its trunk has few small limbs between branches.

+ needles: Linear, 4-sided, blue-green

+ cones: Unisexual on same tree; seed cones yellow to purple-brown; bracts hidden by thin scales notched at tip

+ range: Yukon, British Columbia, and Alberta south to Arizona and New Mexico

Soft and knotty, Engelmann Spruce wood is not prized for lumber, restricted to framing and other unseen construction uses and to paper manufacturing. Instead, it enters the limelight in construction of guitars and piano soundboards. The bark provides tannin, and cord has been made from its branches and roots. Young male cones are eaten raw or cooked, used as flavoring, and added to breads and cereals; the seeds are small but edible. A vitamin C–rich infusion is made from the young shoots. Another, made from the bark, is used to treat respiratory ailments. Various resins have been used to treat eczema.

Red Spruce/He-balsam

Picea rubens H to 148 ft (45 m)

A handsome, medium-size evergreen, the Red Spruce remains one of the most important forest trees in the Northeast, despite having been overexploited for myriad purposes.

KEY FACTS

Crown is conical but broader than in other eastern spruces.

+ **needles:** Four-sided, curved, on all sides of twig, bright green

+ **cones:** Male and female on same tree; seed cones long, egg-shaped, red-brown; scales untoothed

+ **range:** Cape Breton to Ontario, south in mountains to North Carolina

Red Spruce grows in pure stands or with other conifers such as Eastern White Pine, Balsam Fir, and Black Spruce. Light, straight-grained, and resilient, its wood is used in construction and papermaking; its resonance makes it sought after for building guitars, violins, piano soundboards, even organ pipes. Its resin was used into the 20th century in chewing gum (replaced now by a substance from a tropical plant). The buds, foliage, and seeds provide food for small mammals and birds (up to half the diet of a White-winged Crossbill). The Spruce Budworm is especially damaging where this spruce grows with Balsam Fir.

|||||||||||||||||||||||||||||||||||||||||||||||||||||||||||||||||||||||||||||||||||

Sitka Spruce

Picea sitchensis H to 197 ft (60 m)

The largest spruce, the tall, grand Sitka, can be found in its long band of Pacific habitat, from 980 feet (300 m) to sea level, its range inland determined by that of ocean fogs.

KEY FACTS

The trunk base is buttressed.

+ needles: Yellow- to blue-green, sharp, flat, with 2 white bands beneath

+ cones: Male and female on same plant; seed cones cylindrical, hanging from upper shoots; scales thin, irregularly toothed

+ range: Narrow strip along coast from south-central Alaska to northern California

Different parts of the Sitka Spruce have many uses in food, varnish, medicine, and for making rope and cord. The wood is exceptionally strong, thanks to its long, straight grain, especially when its light weight is considered. That combination caught the imagination of airplane designers in both world wars. So did its cost, then less than that of steel or aluminum. It is still used in aerobatic craft. (The largest flying boat ever built was an immense seaplane, made entirely of wood, called the "Spruce Goose"—even though it was made of birch.) Sitka Spruce is a food source for birds and small mammals. It is rarely cultivated.

Jack Pine
Pinus banksiana H to 89 ft (27 m)

Our most northerly ranging pine, the Jack Pine is usually a small to medium-size tree that soon loses the pyramidal form of its youth to assume a more gnarled look.

KEY FACTS

Fire is often needed to open cones.

+ needles: In 2s, olive to gray-green, stiff, curved to slightly twisted; margins rough

+ cones: Crooked toward twig tip; scales thick, stiff, with fragile spine; resinous

+ range: Much of Canada, Great Lakes states, New England, south to Missouri, West Virginia

Large stands of Jack Pine are requisite as breeding habitat for the endangered Kirtland's Warbler (*Setophaga kirtlandii*), which nests almost exclusively in the Lower Peninsula of Michigan, near the southern extent of the tree's range. Historically, fires maintained this open habitat, but now it must be maintained by controlled burning. The tree supplies wood for use as pulp, posts, and firewood. Young trees are a host for the sweet fern blister rust, which causes orange cankers to grow on the trunks, and galls to form on the lower branches. Mature trees are defoliated by the Jack Pine Budworm.

Lodgepole Pine

Pinus contorta H to 98 ft (30 m)

Often found in expansive pure stands, the slender Lodgepole Pine is expected to decline drastically as a result of warming in its cool range, drought, and epidemic levels of Pine Sawyers.

KEY FACTS

Inland, this pine is tall, slender, and straight; in coastal or wet areas, it is shrubby and twisted.

+ needles: In 2s, curved, thick, stiff

+ cones: Broadly oval; scales with curved spine

+ range: Alaska to Baja California; most abundant in northern Rockies and Pacific coast area

American Indians used the slim, flexible limbs to build tepees (thus its common name), the soft inner bark for food, and the sap in medicines. The wood is used in framing, posts, railroad cross ties, and paneling, and to make pulp. It is a close relative of the Jack Pine, with which it hybridizes where the two occur together.

Like its relative, it is plagued by Pine Sawyers; the insects spread fungi, and, girdling the tree, they kill it. But in an odd turn of events, the dead trees provide fuel for fires, enhancing germination of Lodgepole seeds. Seedlings outperform those of other species.

II

Shortleaf Pine
Pinus echinata H 80–100 ft (24–30 m)

The Shortleaf Pine is second in commercial importance (behind Loblolly) in the Southeast, where it is used for turpentine production, plywood, flooring, beams, and pulp.

KEY FACTS

The crown is pyramidal to rounded; the trunk is clear of scrubby limbs.

+ needles: In 2s and 3s, long, slender, dark blue-green

+ cones: Cylindrical, conical, or egg-shaped; scales thin, prickle-tipped

+ range: Southeast; also New York and New Jersey to Missouri, Oklahoma, and Texas

The most wide-ranging yellow pine of the Southeast, the Shortleaf has needles that could be deemed short only in comparison with those of other native southern pines. The branches are irregular, compared with the straighter ones of the Loblolly, with which it hybridizes where their ranges overlap (as it also does with the Pitch Pine). Its seeds provide cover and forage for birds, squirrels, chipmunks, and mice. The Shortleaf's plated bark has resin ducts, appearing as small holes. In addition to Pine Sawyers, it is threatened by littleleaf disease, caused by a root fungus in poorly drained soils.

Piñon Pine/**Two-needle Piñon**
Pinus edulis H to 20 ft (6 m)

A handsome, small, gnarled tree, the Piñon has a dense, rounded, conic crown. Increased droughts have recently killed trees whose habitat is the less dry portion of the species' range.

KEY FACTS

Branches persist almost to the trunk base; the limbless portion is taller, and the silhouette is more irregular with age.

+ needles: In 2s, sometimes 1s or 3s, dark green, curving

+ cones: Spherical; scales lack prickle

+ range: Utah, Arizona, Colorado, New Mexico; small numbers in adjacent states

The seeds of the slow-growing Piñons do not fall when the cone opens. Their dispersal depends on the foraging of Pinyon Jays (named for the tree), which pluck the seeds from the cone scales and then stash them for future eating. Some seeds inevitably go forgotten and eventually germinate. The jays have mammalian competitors. Humans also collect the seeds but do not lose track of them so often. Indigenous peoples have harvesting rights to these traditional foods—called pine nuts in English, *pignoli* in Italian—and there is a commercial harvest. The wood is used as fuel, for posts, and in incenses.

||||||||||||||||||||||||||||||||||||||||||||||||||||||||||||||||||||||||||||||||||||

Slash Pine

Pinus elliottii H 59–100 ft (18–30 m)

Usually inhabiting coastal plains and overgrown swampland, Slash Pines do well in acidic soil and grow fast and so are favorites in reforestation programs.

KEY FACTS

These have a rounded crown and reddish brown bark, becoming plated.

+ **needles:** In 2s or 3s; long, straight, stout

+ **cones:** Long, conical to ovoid, glossy, stalked; scales with outcurved prickle

+ **range:** Coastal Plain of South Carolina to Florida Keys and Louisiana; naturalized in nearby states

A tree of warm, humid flatwoods in poor, sandy Coastal Plain soils, the Slash Pine is grown in suitable areas worldwide for its wood, which is heavy, strong, durable, and compares favorably with that of the Longleaf Pine; its resin is used to make turpentine and rosin. (The species has become invasive in Hawaii and Australia and is under scrutiny in the entire Pacific Rim.) It is like the related Loblolly, except the Slash Pine often has needles in twos (mostly threes in the Loblolly) and larger cones. Large stands are especially hard-hit by the fusiform rust fungus, the most serious disease of pines in the Southeast.

Sugar Pine
Pinus lambertiana H 98–164 ft (30–50 m)

Our largest, most majestic member of the genus *Pinus,* the long-lived Sugar Pine inhabits mainly mixed-conifer forests. It can take 100 years or more to begin producing seeds.

KEY FACTS

This pine grows mostly on damper northern slopes. It has heavy seed cones (largest of any tree), which can weigh down branch tips.

+ **needles:** In 5s, blue-green, straight, slender

+ **cones:** Long, brown (purple when young), long-stalked, hanging

+ **range:** Mountains of Oregon and California

The Sugar Pine takes its name from the sweet-smelling and sweet-tasting resin that oozes from injured wood and forms candy-like beads. It is said to taste better than maple sugar, a trait native peoples took advantage of—though in moderation, because it is a laxative. They also used the resin to affix points and feathers to arrow shafts. The timber is appreciated for its workability, lightness, and strength and is used in framing and molding. Despite the tree's rapid growth rate, it cannot keep pace with harvests. Although it is planted in its native range, it has not been successful in culture elsewhere.

Singleleaf Piñon

Pinus monophylla H 16–66 ft (5–20 m)

The Singleleaf Piñon is often the dominant tree, a key element in the piñon–juniper woodlands of the mountains. As do other piñons, it depends on the Pinyon Jay for dispersal of its seeds.

KEY FACTS

Bark is gray and scaly, developing reddish furrows; the trunk branches to the base.

+ needles: Gray-green to blue-green, mostly solitary; stout, curved, sharp-pointed

+ cones: Broadly egg-shaped; a few woody scales

+ range: Idaho south to California, Nevada, Arizona, and New Mexico

Humans have long eaten the seeds of the Singleleaf Piñon. The seeds are known as pine nuts, but American Indians still roast the cones and grind the seeds to make traditional soups and cakes. This practice was disrupted in the late 1800s, when the resin-rich trees were harvested for use as a fuel in smelting silver. More recently, deemed low-quality forage for livestock, the trees have been destroyed in favor of other species. Other uses are as fence posts and Christmas trees. The parasitic Dwarf Mistletoe affects the Singleleaf, and a number of insects and fungal diseases especially harm piñons.

Western White Pine

Pinus monticola H 45–160 ft (14–49 m)

Closely resembling its relative the Eastern White Pine, this species grows fast and is quick to become established following a disturbance, such as fire.

KEY FACTS

This tall and narrow pine's trunk is clear of scrubby branches.

+ **needles:** In 5s, long, sometimes twisted, blue-green, whitish waxy wash

+ **cones:** Long, narrow cylinders hang from a long stalk; scales thin, curved back

+ **range:** British Columbia to California; Alberta to Nevada and Utah

Primarily a mountain tree, this species ranges to sea level at its northern extent. The wood is light, soft, straight-grained, and nonresinous. Easily worked and excellent for finer products than that of many conifers, it is used in interior details, trims, floors, and for matches and tooth-picks. White Pine blister rust, caused by a fungus native to Asia and introduced into North America via Europe around 1900, attacks the five-needle pines and is especially grave in this species, having killed as much as 90 percent of trees in some regions. Bears, tearing into trunks for the sweet sapwood, also cause irreparable harm.

Longleaf Pine
Pinus palustris H 80–130 ft (24–40 m)

Once widespread, the Longleaf Pine was the keystone of unique habitats of the southeastern Coastal Plain. This grand species has a long life span, and can live for more than 300 years.

KEY FACTS

The needles are longest of our pines; the branches are sparse, relatively short, and stout; the crown is open and asymmetrical.

+ needles: In 3s, slender, flexible, usually hanging

+ cones: Largest of eastern pines; woody, hanging

+ range: Coastal Plain sandhills and flats, Virginia to Texas

As a seedling, the Longleaf Pine passes through a "grass stage" during which it grows thicker instead of taller, and its taproot becomes established; the long needles at this unbranching stage recall tufts of bunchgrasses. Historically, fires created a savanna characterized by the enormous pines and other fire-adapted species. Overharvest (for lumber, pulp, turpentine, and resin, especially for naval purposes), elimination of fires, and management for other species wiped out up to 95 percent of this habitat, but the species and the savannas are being reestablished in much of its former range by extensive plantings maintained by prescribed burning.

Ponderosa Pine

Pinus ponderosa H 60–140 ft (18–39 m)

Our most widely distributed and most abundant pine, the stately Ponderosa gets its name from the Spanish adjective meaning heavy, or ponderous.

KEY FACTS

Mature bark is cinnamon and plated.

+ needles: Mostly in 3s, with tiny teeth on edges, sharp, with turpentine odor

+ cones: Male and female on same tree; seed cones reddish, egg-shaped, not stalked; scales with stout prickles

+ range: Pacific coastal mountains and Rockies

The Ponderosa Pine is found in pure stands and in mixed-conifer forests, where it towers over other trees. One of the most important sources of timber in the West, its wood is used for construction and cabinetmaking, as well as for pulp and firewood. Though sometimes used for Christmas trees, it is not farmed. Larvae of the moth *Chionodes retiniella* feed exclusively on the Ponderosa's needles. Government fire suppression since the early 1900s threatened the Ponderosa's native parklike habitat, because its competitors were no longer killed by the flames. It is now often managed with the aid of controlled burning.

Red Pine/Norway Pine

Pinus resinosa H 50–100 ft (15–30 m)

Norway Pine is a misnomer for this North American native. It was probably so labeled by European explorers and settlers for whom it recalled the Norway Spruce.

KEY FACTS

This pine of cold regions usually towers over other trees; the crown is dense and rounded.

+ needles: In 2s, sometimes twisted, snapping when bent

+ cones: Seed cones near branch tips, small, egg-shaped, not prickly

+ range: Cape Breton Island to Manitoba, around the Great Lakes, south to Virginia

Formerly one of the main timber trees in much of its range, the Red Pine has light, close-grained wood, which is well suited for construction and the manufacture of pulp. As in many pines, the resin is made into turpentine. Vanillin, used in flavorings, is isolated during pulp processing. The tree is often cultivated as an ornamental or as a shade tree, and several cultivars, including a dwarf version, have been developed. Fire is needed to create the condition the seeds need for germination, namely bare mineral soil, and when there are no fires, other species will eventually replace it.

Eastern White Pine
Pinus strobus H 50–220 ft (15–67 m)

The Iroquois tree of peace, the Eastern White Pine once had
extensive stands in the Northeast but has been so exploited that
only one percent of those stands survive.

KEY FACTS

**Branches are tiered,
long, and horizontal.**

+ needles: In 5s, light
green to bluish, edges
rough

+ cones: Seed cones
slim, hanging, stalked;
resinous, and some-
what curved

+ range: Newfound-
land to Manitoba,
around Great Lakes;
New England to West
Virginia; mountains
south to Georgia

The White Pine was already being cut by colonists by
the 1650s, and aggressive logging for the next two
centuries did irreparable damage. The tree provided resins, pitch, and turpentine for use on ships, and its straight,
strong trunks were ideal for ships' masts. Today, the wood
is used in construction and for trim, furniture, and
pulpwood, the demand met by cultivation. Many
cultivars are grown, including dwarf
and weeping varieties. In the
United Kingdom, it is called
the Weymouth Pine, for British
explorer George Weymouth, who
returned in 1605 with seeds he had
collected in what is now Maine.

Loblolly Pine

Pinus taeda H 60–140 ft (18–43 m)

Cultivated varieties of the large, fragrant, and resin-rich Loblolly Pine include a 20-foot version often planted in windscreens; the wild type is not suitable because it sheds its lower branches.

KEY FACTS

This fragrant tree is pyramid-shaped when young, and eventually drops lower branches.

+ **needles:** In 3s, slender, stiff, sometimes slightly twisted

+ **cones:** Seed cones woody; scales thin with short prickle

+ **range:** Mainly in Coastal Plain and Piedmont region from southern New Jersey to eastern Texas

The Loblolly's rapid growth habit is a mixed blessing. The tree is one of the first to be naturally established in abandoned fields and is a good soil stabilizer. It is the most commercially important southern pine, but often at a price. Raised in dense monocultures, it is productive in lumber and forest products and renewable for those purposes, but these tree farms never will revert to the mixed-hardwood stands that they often replaced and that otherwise would develop. Mixed forests sustain greater biodiversity, and their wholesale substitution by depauperate Loblolly stands is receiving attention in restoration projects.

Virginia Pine
Pinus virginiana H 25–49 ft (10–15 m)

Common in the Piedmont and foothills of the Appalachians,
the Virginia Pine has been called the Oldfield Pine because it is
one of the first trees to grow on abandoned agricultural fields.

KEY FACTS

This smallish pine's
limbs grow irregularly
from the trunk, which
often bears stubs of
old branches.

+ **needles:** In 2s,
short, pointed,
twisted, spreading,
serrate

+ **cones:** Seed cones
small, conical to egg-
shaped, woody; scales
with slim, curved
prickle

+ **range:** New York
to Ohio, south to
Mississippi

Thanks to its scrubby look, the Virginia Pine is also
known as Scrub Pine, but its low branches remain on
the tree, which helps make it the most popular species
in the South for use as a Christmas tree. It grows in pure
stands or mixed with various other trees, including hardwoods, which, in nature, will eventually shade it out. The
Virginia Pine pioneers on old fields
and is planted on abandoned
fields and cutover lands. The
wood is often used for pulp or
rough lumber. In older trees,
woodpeckers nest in the trunk,
creating cavities where fungi have
softened the wood.

‖‖

Douglas-fir
Pseudotsuga menziesii H 80–150 ft (24–46 m)

The grand, long-lived Douglas-fir is among the most important of our timber trees. Unlike the upright cones of the true firs, those of the Douglas-fir hang from the branches.

KEY FACTS

Pyramidal when young, the tree loses its lower branches later for a cylindrical appearance.

+ **needles:** Flattened, on slim twigs

+ **cones:** Seed cones with 3-pointed seed bracts projecting beyond the rounded scales

+ **range:** Coast to mountains from British Columbia to California, and to tree line in Rockies

One of the largest trees in the world (unusually can reach 300 feet/92 m), the Douglas-fir produces a great volume of timber, which is used in support beams, interior woodworking, and plywood veneer. The species is used in landscaping, and numerous cultivars have been developed. In fact, the tree is planted as an ornamental in cool regions worldwide, and can be invasive outside its natural range. A variety called the Rocky Mountain Douglas-fir *(P. menziesii* var. *glauca)* is smaller, its foliage with a bluish or grayish cast (i.e., glaucous). Its seed bracts curve back on themselves, pointing toward the cone base.

Eastern Hemlock

Tsuga canadensis H 66–100 ft (20–30 m)

In the southern reaches of its range, the Eastern Hemlock is under attack by the Hemlock Woolly Adelgid, an insect from Asia that feeds on a tree's sap, killing the tree in only a few years.

KEY FACTS

Branches are drooping, with pubescent twigs and fissured bark.

+ needles: Flattened, in 2 ranks

+ cones: Seed cones to 0.8 in (2 cm), egg-shaped, stalked, borne at branch tips

+ range: Ontario to Nova Scotia, Minnesota through northeastern states, to mountains of Georgia and Alabama

The wood is of poor quality, sometimes used in general construction and as pulp. Many cultivars have been developed, including dwarf, shrubby, and weeping forms. The related but geographically distinct Western Hemlock— *T. heterophylla* (H 130–230 ft/40–70 m)—is the largest species of the genus, common and widespread in its range from Alaska to California (especially Oregon and Washington), as well as Montana. Its seed cones are 0.75–1 inch (2–2.5 cm) long, unstalked, its twigs finely pubescent. The hard, durable, and light wood makes it commercially superior to that of other hemlocks. It is rarely cultivated.

Pacific Yew

Taxus brevifolia H 15–50 ft (5–15 m)

A slow-growing evergreen that prefers moist, rocky environments, the Pacific Yew has lithe branches that often appear drooping or weeping.

KEY FACTS

The yew is nonresinous, with thin, reddish brown bark.

+ **leaves:** Flat, pointed; borne spirally but appear in 2 ranks

+ **cones:** Berrylike, one seed surrounded by red, fleshy aril

+ **range:** Alaska to central California in mountains; isolated population from southeastern British Columbia to Idaho

A chemical compound isolated from the Pacific Yew (and found in other yews) is used in chemotherapy for cancer. The compound, known as the generic drug paclitaxel, from the name of the genus, is now manufactured with semisynthetic and cell culture procedures that do not harm the trees. The attractive wood is hard, heavy, strong yet flexible, fine grained, and easily worked. But the supply is limited, and the small size of the trunk and limbs limits their use to such things as canoe paddles, carvings, musical instruments, harpoon and spear handles, archery bows, and firewood. Grown ornamentally, the tree is especially good in hedges.

||||||||||||||||||||||||||||||||||||||||||||||||||||||||||||||||||||||||||||||||||||||||

Common Sumac/Smooth Sumac
Rhus glabra H to 23 ft (7 m)

Common Sumac is a familiar shrub or small tree along roadsides, field edges, and train tracks. In the fall, red leaves and, on female plants, clusters of dark red berries, are its trademark.

KEY FACTS

This fast-growing sumac is nonpoisonous, but is related to Poison Sumac.

+ leaves: Pinnately compound; 7–31 narrow, toothed leaflets

+ flowers/fruits: Male and female inflorescences are on separate plants, at branch ends.

+ range: All 48 contiguous U.S. states and across Canada; most common in East

Common Sumac is popular in gardens for its striking red autumn foliage—giving it another name, Scarlet Sumac. But it can be weedy, spreading via underground stems. It may be confused with its look-alike cousin Poison Sumac (*Toxicodendron vernix*), but the latter is rarely encountered, restricted to moist, even wet areas. Also, in *T. vernix,* male and female flowers grow on the same plant, the leaves have fewer leaflets, and the fruit clusters grow in the axils where two branches diverge. Sumac seeds provide food for birds and insects into the winter, and those of Common Sumac can be made into a lemonade-like beverage.

Pawpaw

Asimina triloba H to 40 ft (12 m)

The Pawpaw has few insect pests, possibly because its leaves contain unsavory chemical compounds. Compounds in the seeds show promise for use in cancer chemotherapy.

KEY FACTS

Colonies are often created by suckering.

+ **leaves:** Alternate, to 1 ft (30 cm) long; oval, narrowing basally

+ **flowers/fruits:** Flowers bell-shaped, 6-petaled, purple; berries fleshy, large, roughly cylindrical, ripening to yellow, then brown

+ **range:** Southern Ontario, eastern states west to Nebraska, Texas

The Pawpaw is a northern representative of the tropical custard apple family. Pawpaws were once harvested, but their supply has dwindled as forests have been cut. The fruit is delicious, but fierce competition from wildlife makes it a prize indeed. Contact with the fruit and leaves can occasionally cause dermatitis. The species is cultivated in its native range, but its wood has no value. The flowers' putrid scent attracts small flies and beetles, which effect pollination. *Asimina* comes from an American Indian name for the tree; the common name probably echoes the Spanish *papayo*, a word of Arawak origin in the West Indies describing a similar but unrelated fruit, the papaya.

American Holly

Ilex opaca H 20–49 ft (6–15 m)

An evergreen broadleaf, the American Holly is a common shrub or small tree of the understory, most common in the humid southeastern United States.

KEY FACTS

This holly sometimes has multiple trunks; bark is smooth and gray.

+ **leaves:** Alternate, oval, stiff, sparsely but strongly toothed; tooth tips sharp

+ **flowers/fruits:** Flowers unisexual, on separate trees, tiny, inconspicuous; fruits orange or red berrylike drupes, often dense

+ **range:** Mainly eastern and southern U.S.

The American Holly is the favorite of the evergreen hollies, with its handsome foliage, pyramidal form, and beautiful berries, ubiquitous in holiday and winter arrangements wherever it grows or is grown. More then 300 cultivars have been developed (but a female tree is needed, with a male nearby, if berries are expected). The berries also provide food for many birds and small mammals, which disperse the seeds. The wood is white and not important as a source of lumber. It is used in veneers, as pulpwood, and in creation of small wooden objects. The slow-growing tree tolerates a range of soil types.

Common Winterberry
Ilex verticillata H 8–15 ft (2.4–4.5 m)

The deciduous Common Winterberry is a popular ornamental and is striking in winter with its red berries borne on bare branches with dark, smooth bark.

KEY FACTS

This small tree is multi-trunked.

+ **leaves:** Alternate, elliptic, pointed; margin toothed, lacking spines

+ **flowers/fruits:** Flowers unisexual, on separate trees; greenish white; fruits bright-red berrylike drupes, often dense

+ **range:** From Quebec to Newfoundland south to Florida and Louisiana

The Common Winterberry is most abundant in wet areas, along streams, and in moist wooded habitats of the Coastal Plain. The red berries lend color to the winter landscape until the birds make off with them. A number of cultivars have been developed, and male and female cultivars must be paired up to ensure that they flower at the same time. The bark of the Winterberry was listed in the U.S. Pharmacopeia for most of the 19th century. Concoctions made from it have been used as an astringent, a bitter tonic, or a febrifuge (thus another of its common names, Feverbush).

Yaupon

Ilex vomitoria H 12–25 ft (3.7–7.6 m)

As in other hollies, the fruits of the Yaupon are an important winter food for birds and small mammals, which distribute the seeds.

KEY FACTS

This evergreen shrub branches heavily inside; can form dense thickets.

+ leaves: Alternate, oval, shiny, thick, small

+ flowers/fruits: Flowers unisexual, on separate plants, inconspicuous, greenish white; fruits bright-red drupes, numerous

+ range: Virginia to Florida, west to Oklahoma and Texas

The Yaupon's species label, *vomitoria,* is a misnomer. Certain American Indian tribes drank a ceremonial infusion that caused purging, and Yaupon was erroneously thought to be the emetic agent. Its twigs and leaves contain caffeine and are used to make a tealike drink not unlike maté, a beverage made from another holly, *I. paraguariensis,* and enjoyed in parts of South America. The name "Yaupon" is from a Catawban word related to the word for tree. This holly, too, is a popular ornamental, used for winter color in the landscape and in holiday decorations; cultivars include dwarf and weeping forms.

Devil's Walkingstick
Aralia spinosa H 15–23 ft (4.6–7 m)

The Devil's Walkingstick is in the Ginseng family, along with the invasive English Ivy, the *Panax* ginsengs, and the popular houseplant Schefflera.

KEY FACTS

This plant bears short, strong spines.

+ leaves: Alternate, to 32 in (81 cm) long, compound to doubly so; leaflets opposite, oval, pointed

+ flowers/fruits: Flowers unisexual, on same plant; tiny, white, in broad clusters; fruits fleshy, black berries

+ range: New Jersey to Florida, west to Texas and Missouri

Though its description may sound menacing, the Devil's Walkingstick is appreciated and even grown ornamentally for its intricate foliage, appealing inflorescences and fruits, and fall color. Its leaves turn bright yellow, and the black fruit are borne in clusters on bright pink stalks. The berries were eaten by the Iroquois, and also provide food for birds and small mammals, as well as black bear. The plant, a shrub or small tree of the understory, often forms dense clusters and has an open, irregular, flat crown. It is aromatic and deciduous, and its bark, roots, and berries have been used medicinally.

||||||||||||||||||||||||||||||||||||||||||||||||||||||||||||||||||||||||||||||||||||

Big Sagebrush

Artemisia tridentata H 2–13 ft (0.6–4 m)

This evergreen member of the Aster family is one of the most wide-ranging shrubs in western North America, a dominant species to the tree line in much of the Great Basin.

KEY FACTS

The shrub is covered with fine gray hairs.

+ leaves: Alternate, wedge-shaped, 3-lobed at tip

+ flowers/fruits: Flowers perfect, tiny, tubular, yellow, in heads of 3–12; fruits seedlike, dry, hard, flat, broadest toward tip

+ range: British Columbia to Baja California, east to the Dakotas

The coarse, aromatic Big Sagebrush is a plant of dry, rocky soils that can live 100 years or longer. While not related to the sages, which are in the mint family, it has an aroma and a growth form that are not unlike those of some sages. Protein-rich (more nutritious than Alfalfa), it serves as forage for many large herbivores, especially in winter. Today it is used mainly as firewood and in smudges and incenses—its aromatic oils burn strongly and fragrantly. Native peoples, too, used it for those purposes but also made ropes and baskets from it and used it medicinally to treat a range of symptoms, as a tea and as a disinfectant.

Red Alder

Alnus rubra H to 60 ft (18 m)

Alnus rubra is our tallest alder and, unlike the others, a commercially viable source of timber. In fact, it is the Pacific Northwest's most important hardwood tree.

KEY FACTS

Inner bark and heartwood are red, thus the common name.

+ leaves: Alternate, oval, pointed, with rounded teeth

+ flowers/fruits: Catkins unisexual, on same plant, in clumps, male drooping, female erect; fruits small cones

+ range: southeastern Alaska to southern California, within 125 miles of Pacific

Native peoples made a red dye from the inner bark and used it to color their fishing nets, which made them less visible to fish. The tree also had medicinal uses, possibly because it contains, as do the willows, aspirin-like chemical compounds that show antitumor properties. Its rapid growth makes it a good pioneer on disturbed lands, which it stabilizes. It is short-lived because when other trees invade, it cannot survive in the resulting shade. Associated with its roots are nitrogen-fixing bacteria, which provide the trees nitrogenous nutrients. The wood is used in furniture, pallets, plywood, spools, and boxes, and in pulp and as firewood.

Hazel Alder

Alnus serrulata H 12–20 ft (3.6–6 m)

Primarily an Atlantic coastal species, the Hazel Alder is a common large shrub or small tree of moist lowlands and stream banks, where it is mostly found in mixed stands.

KEY FACTS

This alder can be spindly with crooked trunks.

+ **leaves:** Alternate, oval, edge wavy, finely serrate

+ **flowers/fruits:** Catkins unisexual, on same plant, male pendent, female erect; fruits small, woody cones, lasting into winter

+ **range:** Nova Scotia and New Brunswick to Florida, west to Oklahoma and Texas

The Hazel Alder's growth habit makes the tree a superior colonizer and ideal in restoring wetlands, stabilizing stream banks, and mitigating storm-water runoff. When it is sold, it is generally for such purposes. The plant has an extensive root system and forms broad thickets by suckering. The roots are extensive and have symbiotic bacteria that fix nitrogen, providing the tree with nitrogenous nutrients. It is an important component of the American Woodcock's habitat and provides food and shelter for many other birds and small mammals. White-tailed Deer browse on the plants. The tree has had a range of medicinal uses, including as a pain reliever during childbirth.

Yellow Birch

Betula alleghaniensis H 60–75 ft (18–23 m)

The largest and most important birch, this species provides 75 percent of the birch wood used in the United States, and half of the species' entire stock is in Quebec.

KEY FACTS

Yellow-bronze bark (hence the common name) has horizontal lenticels.

+ leaves: Alternate, sharp-tipped, toothed

+ flowers/fruits: Catkins unisexual, on same tree, male pendent, female upright; fruits cone-like

+ range: Southeastern Canada; northeastern U.S., Great Lakes states, south in mountains to Georgia

A species of lower elevations, the Yellow Birch is a slow-growing, long-lived, single-trunked tree. When solitary, it develops a broad, open shape; when crowded, the trees grow tall and slender. The leaves turn a brilliant yellow in the fall. Deer and moose browse on the plants, and birds eat the seeds. A syrup is sometimes derived from the sap, and a tea is made from the twigs or inner bark, which have the aroma and flavor of wintergreen. The dark reddish brown to creamy-white wood is durable and heavy and is used widely in interior finishes, veneers, flooring, furniture, and cabinets.

River Birch

Betula nigra H 50–70 ft (15–21 m)

The fast-growing, shade-intolerant River Birch is a vigorous pioneer species that stabilizes soil on stream banks. The largest specimens grow in the Mississippi Valley.

KEY FACTS

The bark of young trees sheds in papery coils.

+ **leaves:** Alternate, broad, strongly serrate, pointed, wedge-shaped at base

+ **flowers/fruits:** Catkins unisexual, on same tree, male pendent, female upright; fruits cone-like

+ **range:** New Hampshire west to Minnesota, south to northern Florida and west to Texas

The lithe River Birch is the only spring-fruiting birch and the only birch whose native range includes the southeastern Coastal Plain. When young, it has a pyramidal shape, which becomes rounder with age. It often has multiple and highly branching trunks. Most common in floodplains and wet areas, it also grows in drier locations. Though the wood is close grained and sturdy, it is too knotty to be of much commercial value. It is used for furniture, baskets, small objects, and pulpwood. But it is an attractive tree, used as an ornamental; a number of cultivars have been developed. The sap has been concentrated for use as a sweetener.

Water Birch

Betula occidentalis H 20–35 ft (6–11 m)

The Water Birch is a shrub or small tree of wet, wooded sites, often growing near waterways or on banks, occurring sporadically throughout its range.

KEY FACTS

Bark is not exfoliating.

+ **leaves:** Alternate, rounded to wedge-shaped, with small marginal serrations on the larger teeth

+ **flowers/fruits:** Catkins unisexual, on same tree, male pendent, female erect; fruits are cones

+ **range:** In the west, especially in the Rocky Mountains, east to northwestern Ontario

The crown of the Water Birch is irregular and open; the branches are slender and drooping; and it usually has multiple trunks, forming thickets. The tree is too small to have much timber value, but its hard and heavy wood does find utility as posts and firewood. It is seldom cultivated but is planted as a stabilizer and buffer along stream banks; it is rather shade tolerant. Water Birch is an important component in wildlife habitat, and large mammals browse on the plants. Native peoples used a tea prepared from the tree as a diuretic and as a treatment for kidney stones.

Paper Birch/White Birch

Betula papyrifera H 50–70 ft (15–21 m)

The bark of the Paper Birch eventually becomes chalky white and papery, with prominent black lenticels, peeling off in horizontal strips to reveal orange beneath.

KEY FACTS

Pyramidal when young, but shape becomes less regular with age.

+ **leaves:** Alternate, oval, pointed; margins doubly toothed

+ **flowers/fruits:** Catkins unisexual, on same tree; fruits are cones

+ **range:** Alaska to Labrador, south into Rockies, Plains states, and Pennsylvania to North Carolina in mountains

For most of us, the Paper Birch is the tree that probably comes to mind when we think of birch trees, because of its beauty and because it is the most widespread of our birches. It can have one or multiple trunks. A number of cultivars have been developed. The wood is soft but moderately heavy and so is used for fuel, as well as in veneers, plywood, cabinets, furniture, and pulp. The tree's buds, catkins, and seeds provide food for many small mammals and birds, and a range of larger mammals find food in the bark and stems, including moose and porcupines.

Virginia Roundleaf Birch/Ashe's Birch

Betula uber H to 40 ft (12 m)

The first tree species listed as endangered by the U.S., the Virginia Roundleaf Birch is now listed federally as threatened (though still deemed endangered in Virginia, where it is endemic).

KEY FACTS

When crushed, the twigs smell of wintergreen; the bark eventually splits into ragged plates.

+ leaves: Alternate, round to oval, with heart-shaped base, serrate

+ flowers/fruits: Catkins unisexual, on same tree, male pendent, female erect; cones erect

+ range: Endemic to a site in Smyth County, Virginia

The majestic Virginia Roundleaf Birch was first described in 1918, but it was not seen again and was believed extirpated until 1975, when a stand of 41 mature trees was found on a creek bank in Smyth County, Virginia. Thanks to propagation programs, in 2006, the count stood at 961, including 8 trees from the original 1975 group. In 1918, the species was described as a botanical variety of the Sweet Birch (*B. lenta*) but was elevated to its own species in 1945, a decision that is still debated. The 1975 rediscovery went mainstream with a feature in the *New Yorker* the following January.

Southern Catalpa/Indian Bean Tree

Catalpa bignonioides H 25–45 ft (7–14 m)

One of the South's trademark trees, the Southern Catalpa is the host plant of a Sphinx Moth larva, the Catawba Worm, a popular bait for bream; the tree is also called Catawba and Fish Bait tree.

KEY FACTS

This tree can be wider than tall.

+ **leaves:** Opposite or whorled, large, rounded or heart-shaped

+ **flowers/fruits:** Flowers perfect, tubular, 2-lipped, 5-lobed, white, in showy clusters, throat with yellow and purple; fruits slender, beanlike pods

+ **range:** Georgia to Florida, west to Mississippi

The Southern Catalpa has been planted beyond its natural range for shade, beauty, and interest almost since its initial discovery by colonists, but drawbacks to some people are its falling flowers, unpleasant smell, large leaves, seedpods, and the tendency to sucker. It has become naturalized in those areas. The Northern Catalpa, *C. speciosa*, is the most north-ranging member of its family, with a limited natural range that includes southwestern Indiana and southern Illinois, Tennessee, and Arkansas. It is a larger tree, 75–100 feet (23–30 m), with larger leaves; smaller, fewer, and somewhat less attractive flowers; and thicker and longer pods.

Saguaro

Carnegiea gigantea H 40-60 ft (12-18 m)

The unforgettable shape of this tree-size cactus instantly brings to mind the Old West, an association that is exploited in movies and advertisements.

KEY FACTS

The trunk and branches are ribbed, with dense clusters of spines.

+ **leaves:** None

+ **flowers/fruits:** Flowers open at night, crown of white petals with yellow center, 3 in (7.5 cm) across, near branch ends; fruits oval, red, sweet; up to 4,000 seeds

+ **range:** Sonoran Desert in Arizona and into California

Our largest cactus does not develop its trademark upcurved arms until its 75th year; until then, the columnar plant is called a "spear." It can live 200 years. When it rains, the plant absorbs water and physically expands, then uses the water as needed. The cactus grows faster in areas with more rainfall. Its waxy coating helps conserve water. The Saguaro offers nesting habitat to birds including the Gila Woodpecker, Cactus Wren, and Pygmy Owl, and its seeds and fruit provide food. Arizona law makes it a crime to harm a Saguaro, and a permit is required to move one in order to build.

Jumping Cholla

Cylindropuntia fulgida H to 12 ft (3.6 m)

The name "Jumping Cholla" reflects the ease with which the spiny joints separate from the plant when bumped, sticking to one's clothes or skin, seemingly having jumped from the plant.

KEY FACTS

This shrubby cactus has one low-branching trunk.

+ leaves: Reduced to spines

+ flowers/fruits: Flowers pink to magenta, at branch and old fruit tips; 5–8 petals; fruits green, pear-shaped, many-seeded berries

+ range: Sonoran Desert in California and Arizona into New Mexico, Nevada, and Utah

The drooping branches of the Jumping Cholla are jointed, with cylindrical segments. When a fruit persists into the following year, a flower and another fruit can form at its tip, creating a chain of 25 years' worth of end-to-end fruits. This habit gives the plant another name, the Hanging Chain Cholla. The segments are armed with sharp, strong spines in crowded tufts. Because the segments disconnect easily, the ground at the base of the plant is often littered with plant parts, which can take root and form new plants. The fruits and seeds are food sources, especially for rodents, and the flesh of the plant provides water for desert animals, especially during droughts.

Roughleaf Dogwood

Cornus drummondii H 15–25 ft (4.6–7.6 m)

The Roughleaf is a dogwood whose flower clusters are not surrounded by large showy bracts, which may surprise those of us who think of the bracts as the symbol of dogwoods.

KEY FACTS

This dogwood can be a small tree or a multiple-trunked shrub.

+ leaves: Opposite, simple, entire; rough above

+ flowers/fruits: Flowers perfect, with 4 short, off-white petals, in clusters at branch tips; fruits hard berry-like drupes, white, in clusters

+ range: Great Plains, Midwest, Mississippi Valley

The Roughleaf Dogwood is a common component in the understory of rich woodlands. Though not showy, it is nonetheless attractive and has found uses in hedges and borders, around patios and in foundation plantings, and in parking lots and medians. As with many of its relatives, its fruits are eaten and its seeds are dispersed by many birds. And its suckering habit, resulting in those multiple trunks, is helpful in controlling erosion and in buffers. In the leaves, the veins come off the midrib, then arc toward the tip, and eventually nearly parallel with the margin, a dogwood trait.

Flowering Dogwood

Cornus florida H 15–35 ft (4.5–11 m)

In 2012, the United States sent 3,000 saplings of the Flowering Dogwood to Japan to mark the 100th anniversary of the famous cherry trees in Washington, D.C., a gift from Japan in 1912.

KEY FACTS

The branching is often tiered, with limbs to the ground.

+ **leaves:** Opposite, red in fall

+ **flowers/fruits:** Flowers perfect, tiny, in heads surrounded by 4 large white or pink petal-like bracts notched at the tip; fruits red, ovoid drupes

+ **range:** Mainly the eastern half of the U.S.

An eye-catching tree of the understory, the Flowering Dogwood is one of our most beautiful trees. But dogwood anthracnose, a fungal disease discovered in the United States in 1978, has spread throughout its range, causing significant losses of wild and planted trees, especially at higher altitudes and in shadier or moister sites. It first attacks leaves and stems, which die back, then it causes cankers, and the trees die. Guidelines are available for mediating the disease, and the many cultivars include a number of anthracnose-resistant varieties. The hard, dense wood has been used for golf club heads, mallets, tool handles, jewelry boxes, and spools.

Pacific Dogwood
Cornus nuttallii H 30–45 ft (9–14 m)

The drupes of the Pacific Dogwood are eaten and their seeds dispersed by birds and small mammals, as in other dogwoods. Large herbivores browse on the young plants.

KEY FACTS

This dogwood can bloom a second time, in early fall.

+ leaves: Opposite, simple, oval, hairy

+ flowers/fruits: Perfect, tiny flowers, in crowded heads with 4–8 showy, white to pinkish, petal-like bracts; fruits berrylike drupes, pink to red or orange

+ range: Pacific coast, British Columbia to California

The graceful Pacific Dogwood is a striking tree of the Pacific coast, where it is found inland to about 200 miles. It is much like the Flowering Dogwood, with its "flowers" of a small inflorescence and showy bracts. The Pacific Dogwood's flowers are larger, their bracts lack a terminal notch, and the two species' ranges are widely distinct. Anthracnose plagues the Pacific Dogwood; low air circulation and too much water worsen it. Dogwoods are sometimes called cornels, a name referring to their genus. The name is probably derived from the Greek *kerasos,* or "cherry tree," presumably because of the color of the drupes. A few cultivars are available.

Common Persimmon

Diospyros virginiana H 30–40 ft (9–12 m)

When fully ripe (following a solid frost, or if aged beyond technically ripe), a wild persimmon is delicious, tasting somewhat like a date. Earlier, it is so bitter and astringent as to be inedible.

KEY FACTS

Bark forms plates recalling charcoal briquettes.

+ leaves: Alternate, simple, entire, oval

+ flowers/fruits: Male and female flowers on separate trees; female, white, bell-shaped; male clustered, tubular, smaller; fruits fleshy, round, orange to purplish

+ range: East; southern, but found to Connecticut

Persimmons persist on the tree long after the leaves have fallen, which makes them one of the latest available wild fruits. This was nicely timed with the harvest feasts of American Indians and European settlers alike, so persimmons were served. The fruits are eaten fresh and are made into cakes, puddings, breads, candies, pies, jams, and beverages. Humans must vie with raccoons, other mammals, and birds to get the prized fruits. A member of the ebony family, the persimmon has dark, heavy, close-grained wood, which is used in heads for golf club woods, in lathe work, and in carving. Several cultivars have been developed.

||||||||||||||||||||||||||||||||||||||||||||||||||||||||||||||||||||||||||||||||||

Mountain Laurel

Kalmia latifolia H 3–23 ft (1–7 m)

The blight that decimated the American Chestnut in the early 1900s benefited the Mountain Laurel, which prospered as sunlight gained entry to the once denser reaches of the forest.

KEY FACTS

This evergreen broad-leaf shrub is dense and gnarled.

+ **leaves:** Alternate, elliptic, leathery

+ **flowers/fruits:** Flowers perfect, white to pink clusters; 5 petals, fused into saucer shape; fruits small, round, capsules with withered pistil

+ **range:** East of a line from New Brunswick to Louisiana

The Mountain Laurel grows mostly in rounded stands sprawling on the forest floor. It is one of our most magnificent native shrubs (occasionally reaching tree size), common in the wild, and is planted for its showy beauty in yards and parks. Many cultivars have been developed. The stamens are held under tension by the petals, springing loose when tripped by a bee, peppering the insect with pollen, which it transfers to other flowers. All parts of the plant are toxic. It was used among native peoples as a means of suicide, as well as a source of a yellow-brown dye.

Sourwood

Oxydendrum arboreum H 40–60 ft (12–18 m)

The Sourwood finds many uses in landscaping, thanks especially to its leaves, whose vivid fall color has few rivals and which persist longer than most other leaves.

KEY FACTS

The branches often extend to the ground and droop.

+ leaves: Alternate, vivid orange or red in fall

+ flowers/fruits: Flowers cup-shaped, small, white, in spikes along one side of stem, showy; fruits are capsules, silver-gray in fall

+ range: Southeast; west to Kentucky, south to the Gulf and northern Florida

This narrow, small to medium-size tree of the understory has a graceful, open, and irregular shape. It was being cultivated as early as the mid-1700s, and cultivars have been developed. In nature, it is found in mixed stands on drier, upland, wooded sites, often with other heaths (as members of its family are known), such as *Rhododendron* species. It is sensitive to air pollution. The Cherokee and Catawba used the young trees to make arrows, and though the Sourwood's dense, close-grained wood has been used for paneling, fuel, and pulp, it has not had great commercial success.

Sparkleberry/Farkleberry
Vaccinium arboreum H 12–28 ft (3.6–8.5 m)

The Sparkleberry is our only tree-high *Vaccinium,* though some Highbush Blueberries come close. It is more tolerant of more alkaline soils than are its relatives.

KEY FACTS

The tree is spindly with twisted branches and is mostly evergreen.

+ **leaves:** Mostly evergreen, alternate, rounded, leathery, bright red in fall

+ **flowers/fruits:** Flowers white, bell-shaped, 5-lobed, in drooping clusters; fruits black, shiny

+ **range:** Southeast from Virginia to Missouri, to Florida and Texas

The name "Sparkleberry" probably refers to the fruit's shininess; "Farkleberry" may be a play on that name. The fruits are dry, bitter, and mostly ignored. The name has been tied to two Arkansas governors: Orval Eugene Faubus was nicknamed "Farkleberry" by a cartoonist who found it apt for satirizing Faubus and the state's politics. Frank White was dubbed "Governor Farkleberry" after saying that his family had been so poor they had to eat Farkleberries. This attractive plant provides habitat and food for wildlife, and the bark, peeling in red, gray, and brown patches and often splotched with lichen, adds visual interest.

Blueberries

Vaccinium species H various, to 16 ft (5 m)

Though these plants have provided food for humans and wildlife for centuries, cultivars have been developed that provide plumper, juicier, and sweeter berries.

KEY FACTS

Blueberries are mostly upright, small shrubs.

+ leaves: Deciduous or evergreen, oval to tapering at ends

+ flowers/fruits: Flowers bell-shaped, 5-lobed, white, pink, or red, in clusters at end of branches; fruits are blue berries

+ range: Arctic Circle south, especially in cooler areas

The genus *Vaccinium* includes 450 to 500 species of shrubs, vines, and small trees mainly in cooler areas of the Americas, Europe, and Asia, but also in southern Africa, Madagascar, and Hawaii. The "typical" blueberries are endemic to North America. Their classification is difficult. Genetic and molecular studies are incomplete, there are different schools of thought, and hybridization is a further complication. The genus includes the important Highbush (*V. corymbosum*), Lowbush (*V. angustifolium*), Velvetleaf (*V. myrtilloides*), and Rabbiteye (*V. virgatum*) Blueberries and at least nine others, including the Cranberry (*V. macrocarpon*), a low-growing evergreen in acidic bogs in the Northeast.

Mimosa/Silktree

Albizia julibrissin H 20–50 ft (6–15 m)

A native of Asia, from Iran to Japan, the exotic Mimosa was introduced here as an ornamental in the 1700s. It remains popular in gardens, yet it is invasive on roadsides and in disturbed areas.

KEY FACTS

Flowers are borne at branch ends; trunks are often multiple.

+ leaves: Opposite, large, twice compound, feather-like; leaflets opposite

+ flowers/fruits: Flowers pink filamentous pompons, fragrant, clustered; fruits are thin, flat pods

+ range: Nonnative; widely naturalized, invasive, especially in Southeast

The Mimosa is vase-shaped, with a crown of large, feathery leaves. It has bacteria in its roots that can change inert atmospheric nitrogen into forms that can serve as plant nutrients. Wildlife eats its fruit and disperses its many seeds. The roots or an old stump can send up sprouts. As a result, and because it is nonnative, it has no natural enemies to keep it in check, and it is often invasive. The University of Florida Center for Aquatic and Invasive Plants suggests native alternatives, such as Serviceberry (*Amelanchier arborea*), Redbud (*Cercis canadensis*), and Fringe Tree (*Chionanthus virginicus*), but people still plant the Mimosa, and there are many cultivars.

Yellow Paloverde

Parkinsonia microphylla H to 25 ft (7.6 m)

The Yellow Paloverde is a trademark shrub or small tree of the Arizona desert. Its branches are photosynthetic, which gives it a yellow-green cast and its common name.

KEY FACTS

The branches are erect, not flowing.

+ leaves: Alternate, twice compound; 2 leaflets; secondary leaflets tiny, oval, soon dropping

+ flowers/fruits: Flowers perfect, in small clusters; 5 petals—4 yellow, 1 white; fruits are pods constricted between seeds

+ range: Sonoran Desert in California and Arizona

Like its relative the Jerusalem Thorn, the Yellow Paloverde is drought deciduous: It loses its leaves in the hottest and driest part of the year, which lessens water loss. It will even drop some branches if weather is especially severe. It is a "nurse plant" to the Saguaro; the cactus's seeds germinate in its shade, and it protects the seedlings from wind and trampling. Yellow Paloverde wood is used mainly as fuel, and it is cultivated in other arid regions. Buffelgrass *(Cenchrus ciliaris)* was introduced from Africa to grow as food for livestock, but it has become invasive and harms the Yellow Paloverde by robbing it of scarce water from the soil.

Eastern Redbud

Cercis canadensis H 15–28 ft (4.6–8.5 m)

The Eastern Redbud stages a striking display in spring, its pink flowers appearing before most trees have leafed out. Flowers are borne on all parts of the tree, even the trunk.

KEY FACTS

The flower, as in many legumes, recalls that of the familiar garden pea.

+ **leaves:** Alternate, simple, entire, heart-shaped, papery, pendent; yellow in fall

+ **flowers/fruits:** Flowers perfect, pink, stalked, in clusters of 4–8; fruits flat, hanging pods

+ **range:** Eastern half of the U.S.

The Eastern Redbud is not native to what is now Canada; *canadensis* in the scientific name refers to a rather different Canada, a French colony that extended into what is now the U.S., including areas where the Redbud is native. This graceful, often multistemmed shrub or small tree grows on a range of soils and in different light regimes, which, with its beauty at flowering time, have made it a successful ornamental. Cultivars include white-flowered varieties. The tree is too small to be a commercial lumber source. Like many leguminous plants, the Redbud can fix nitrogen.

Honeylocust

Gleditsia triacanthos H 30–80 ft (9–24 m)

The large, forked thorns on the trunk and lower branches of the Honeylocust have been used as pins or even nails. Thornless cultivars are popular in landscaping.

KEY FACTS

The bark becomes ridged, its edges curling.

+ **leaves:** Once or twice compound; leaflets oval

+ **flowers/fruits:** Flowers in hanging unisexual clusters on same tree (some flowers perfect), yellow-green, fragrant; fruits twisting, leathery pods, turning brownish

+ **range:** Midwestern and south-central U.S.

The wood of the Honeylocust is of good quality and durable when in contact with the soil. It is used to make furniture, interior finishings, and utilitarian products such as posts and firewood. The seedpods provide a sweet pulp (thus the common name) that was eaten by native peoples and has been fermented into a beer. The inconspicuous flowers are a source of pollen and nectar for honey. Pharmacognosists have isolated chemical compounds from the tree that have anticancer properties or that show promise in treating rheumatoid arthritis. The pods, bark, and young shoots are often eaten by mammals, the seeds by birds.

Kentucky Coffeetree

Gymnocladus dioicus H 60–80 ft (18–24 m)

The stout branches of the Kentucky Coffeetree lose their leaves early and so can go leafless for half the year. *Gymnocladus* means "naked branch."

KEY FACTS

The bark is fissured with scaly ridges.

+ leaves: Huge, twice compound; leaflets oval, pointed

+ flowers/fruits: Flowers fragrant, in upright clusters; 5 petals and calyx lobes, alternating, greenish white, sexes on same tree; fruits broad, leathery

+ range: Midwest to Appalachians, south to Louisiana

Though the Kentucky Coffeetree is widespread and tolerates a range of conditions, it is not common. Animals that might have dispersed its large seeds—Mastodon, Mammoth, and Giant Sloth—are long extinct, which may have curbed the tree's population. Colonists roasted and milled the seeds to make a coffee-like beverage, but the unroasted seeds are toxic. The drink contains no caffeine and was forgotten when coffee beans became available. In landscaping, male trees are usually used because females drop one part after another, which must be cleaned up. The males, however, lack the interesting pods in winter.

Honey Mesquite/Glandular Mesquite

Prosopis glandulosa H 20–30 ft (6–9 m)

Though only a large shrub or small tree (at its biggest in areas of highest moisture), the Honey Mesquite is still the largest tree in much of its range.

KEY FACTS

It has feathery foliage and long, paired spines.

+ leaves: Alternate, twice compound, smooth, with 2 leaflets, each with small leaflets

+ flowers/fruits: Flowers perfect, white to yellow, fragrant, in spikes; fruits are long cylindrical pods, constricted between seeds

+ range: Central Texas to California

Before Europeans introduced livestock, mesquites may have had more clearly defined ranges. Animals that eat the pods disperse the seed, and have thus blurred the boundaries. In addition to seeds, the Honey Mesquite reproduces by sprouting from the roots. It has found many uses and is being eyed as a promising species for the world's food supply (as well as for animal feed and building materials). Native peoples used the pods for food and to make alcoholic beverages and flour. Mesquite honey is prized for its flavor. Yet where stock is grazed, mesquites are considered weeds and are often destroyed.

Velvet Mesquite
Prosopis velutina H to 30 ft (9 m)

Overgrazing removed range plants that served as fuels in natural fires. Coupled with dispersal of its seeds by livestock, mesquite expanded into grazing lands, where it is considered a pest.

KEY FACTS

Larger than other mesquites, it is spiny, with feathery foliage.

+ **leaves:** Alternate, twice compound, velvety, 2 leaflets, each with smaller leaflets

+ **flowers/fruits:** Flowers perfect, creamy, fragrant, in spikes; fruits are long cylindrical pods, constricted between seeds

+ **range:** Central and southern Arizona

Mesquites such as the Velvet were essential to native peoples of the Southwest. The trees often grew in bosques (wooded assemblages that extended for miles along rivers), allowing the fruit to be gathered almost as if it had been planted. The beans were dried and ground into flour that was used to make bread, a dietary staple; the pods are about 25 percent sugar, and the seeds are high in protein. The trees were also important for articles of everyday life, such as tools, rope, baskets, and weapons. The original extent of the mesquite bosques is diminishing as the mesquites are cut for wood and cleared for agricultural and other development.

Black Locust

Robinia pseudoacacia H 30–60 ft (9–18 m)

The roots of the Black Locust have nodules that contain bacteria capable of fixing nitrogen, that is, of transforming inert nitrogen gas in the air into chemical forms that plants can use.

KEY FACTS

Most leaves have a pair of thorns at the base.

+ leaves: Alternate, compound, feathery; entire, large, oval leaflets

+ flowers/fruits: White, fragrant flowers, typical pea flower, in large, showy, hanging clusters; fruits are flat pods, sometimes persisting

+ range: Central Appalachians and Ozarks

The Black Locust's many seeds and ability to sprout from its roots enable it to establish quickly, even on poor soils—ideal in reclamation projects and erosion control, but not so much in a garden. Nevertheless, it has been widely planted and is naturalized in the 48 contiguous states and much of Canada. It grows (and can be invasive) in many parts of the world, sometimes farmed as an alternative to taking tropical woods. It produces a strong, hard wood used in boats (instead of teak), furniture, paneling, and flooring, in addition to more utilitarian uses including the manufacture of charcoal.

American Chestnut

Castanea dentata H to 100 ft (30 m) before the blight

"Not only was baby's crib likely made of chestnut, but chances were, so was the old man's coffin," George H. Hepting in "Death of the American Chestnut" (*Journal of Forest History*, 1974).

KEY FACTS

The tree is spreading and dense.

+ **leaves:** Alternate, 5–8 in (13–20 cm), pointed; base rounded; margin sharp-toothed

+ **flowers/fruits:** Flowers unisexual, both sexes on same plant—male in catkins, female near catkin bases; fruits spiny capsules with 3 nuts

+ **range:** Eastern United States, Ontario

The American Chestnut has been called the ideal tree. Majestic, massive, it made up 25 to 50 percent of the hardwoods in its range. Its wood was unequalled, it was a key source of tannins used in tanning leather, and the nuts had a ready market in the East. But a fungus, brought from Asia around 1900, caused a blight that destroyed nearly all mature chestnuts in 40 years. The species survives in unaffected areas to which it had been transplanted. Also, the root systems did not succumb and send up sprouts. Studies are under way to exploit what natural resistance exists, and to explore hybridization with a resistant chestnut from China.

American Beech

Fagus grandifolia H to 66 ft (20 m)

No matter how remote the tree, it seems initials will be found carved into the trunk of an American Beech, the carving sealed by the bark and remaining for posterity.

KEY FACTS

The smooth bark is light gray.

+ leaves: Alternate, to 5.5 in (14 cm), pointed; margin toothed

+ flowers/fruits: Flowers unisexual, male in round heads, female 2–4 in spikes, on same tree; fruits spiny husks with 2 3-faced, winged nuts

+ range: New Brunswick to Florida to Mississippi Valley

The American Beech is a large, imposing, slow-growing, and long-lived tree usually found in mixed hardwood forests, where it is the dominant or a codominant tree, sturdy and with many branches. The tree is deciduous, but many leaves persist through the winter, their light reddish brown somehow almost showy against the gray bark. The nuts are delicious, but competitors are many, including squirrels, chipmunks, mice, raccoons, porcupines, opossums, rabbits, deer, black bears, and foxes, not to mention Ruffed Grouse, turkeys, bobwhites, and pheasants. Beech wood is used in furniture, veneers, and flooring, and for fence posts and fuel.

White Oak

Quercus alba H to 82 ft (25 m)

The White Oak is possibly our most abundant tree, usually dominant when present, and our most commercially important of the 58 species of oak in North America north of Mexico.

KEY FACTS

The leaves are red-purple in fall.

+ leaves: Alternate, to 7 in (18 cm); 7–10 rounded lobes

+ flowers/fruits: Flowers in unisexual catkins on same tree; male lax, green-yellow; female reddish, in leaf axils; acorn caps cover a third of nut

+ range: Southern Ontario and Quebec to eastern and central U.S.

The White Oak is usually found in mixed hardwood forests. Half of U.S. hardwood production is White Oak, because of its quality and abundance. It is used in furnishings, interiors, shipbuilding, and wine and whiskey barrels. This tree is the flagship of the White Oak group, whose acorns mature the first year on new branches. The inside of the acorn shell is not hairy, and the cap's scales are brown and flat. The meat is sweet to somewhat bitter. The leaf lobes are rounded and do not have bristles at the tip. The bark is often pale gray and blocky. Species of the White Oak group will hybridize with one another.

Arizona White Oak
Quercus arizonica H to 60 ft (18 m)

The Arizona White Oak is found in arid and semiarid areas in oak and piñon woodlands, growing larger in areas with more moisture, such as canyons.

KEY FACTS

The trunk is short, and the branches are twisted.

+ leaves: Evergreen or nearly so, alternate, to 3.5 in (9 cm) thick

+ flowers/fruits: Catkins typically oak; acorns oblong, to 1 in (2.5 cm); caps cover a third of nut

+ range: Central Arizona to southwestern New Mexico into Texas

The long-lived Arizona White Oak (White Oak group) is a shrub to a medium-size tree, yet one of the largest of the southwestern oaks. It has stout, spreading branches and an irregular crown, and its light gray bark can be an inch (2.5 cm) thick on a mature tree. The acorns are eaten by cattle and deer, but they are not the preferred acorn. Birds forage in the stands, and deer browse on the sprouts. The wood is neither straight enough nor large enough to provide commercial timber, and, though difficult to cut and work, it is used for fuel and sometimes in furniture.

Scarlet Oak

Quercus coccinea H to 100 ft (30 m)

The Scarlet Oak is widely planted in the U.S., Canada, and Europe as an ornamental and a shade tree, and cultivars have been developed. The leaves turn brilliant red in autumn.

KEY FACTS

The trunk of this oak swells at the base.

+ **leaves:** Alternate, to 6 in (15 cm); 5- to 9-lobed, each with a bristled tip; sinuses are deep and C-shaped

+ **flowers/fruits:** Catkins typically oak; acorns to 1.2 in (3 cm); caps cover half of nut

+ **range:** Eastern and central U.S.

The Scarlet Oak (a member of the Red Oak group; see Northern Red Oak, p. 98) is a large, fast-growing tree with stout, upright, spreading branches and an open, rounded crown, the bark thin and gray-black. It is common in dry upland forests, where it grows in large pure stands and mixed stands. The wood is reddish brown, coarse-grained, and strong, inferior to that of the Northern Red Oak but, as wood of many other species of the Red Oak group, is marketed as Red Oak. It is used as lumber. Small mammals and birds use the acorns and seedlings as food, and the trees provide nesting sites, including cavities.

Coastal Sage Scrub Oak
Quercus dumosa H 3–7 ft (1–2 m)

The Coastal Sage Scrub Oak usually grows within sight of the Pacific Ocean—that is, on prime real estate. The tree, which has never been common, is at great risk from human encroachment.

KEY FACTS

The tree has a scraggly look.

+ leaves: Evergreen or nearly so, to 1 in (2.5 cm), irregularly toothed or shallowly lobed, with erect curly hairs on underside

+ flowers/fruits: Catkins typically oak; acorns narrow, pointed; reddish caps cover a third of the nut

+ range: Southern California

Most Coastal Sage Scrub Oaks of the White Oak group (see White Oak) have at one time been considered *Quercus dumosa*, but the species concept is now much narrower. It refers to a plant growing in a limited part of southern California and restricted to Coastal Sage Scrub habitats. Most trees once considered this species are now included as the more widespread and common California Scrub Oak, *Q. berberidifolia*, which ranges to the high north coast mountains and to the foothills of the Sierra Nevada. Its acorns are more rounded, and its leaves lack hairs on the underside. Its range does not overlap with that of *Q. dumosa*.

Southern Red Oak
Quercus falcata H to 100 ft (30 m)

A medium-size to large tree, the Southern Red Oak is also known as Spanish Oak, probably because it grows in some of the former Spanish colonies.

KEY FACTS

Its trunk is straight, its crown rounded.

+ leaves: Alternate, to 9 in (23 cm); 3–7 lobes, terminal longest, sharp, often curved; sinuses deep, U-shaped

+ flowers/fruits: Catkins typically oak; acorns round, orangish, 0.5 in (1.3 cm); caps cover a third of nut

+ range: Southeast to southern Missouri, eastern Texas

The Southern Red Oak (a member of the Red Oak group; see Northern Red Oak, p. 98) is a handsome tree that is rather fast growing and fairly long lived. It grows on dry, poor, sandy, upland soils. The bark is dark and thick with deep furrows between broad, scaly ridges. It is an important timber tree, providing light-red wood that is coarse grained, hard, and strong. It is used in furniture, cabinets, veneer, and for pulp and fuel. Native peoples used oaks for myriad medicinal purposes. The Southern Red Oak was used to treat such conditions as indigestion, chapped skin, and fever, and as an antiseptic and tonic.

Gambel Oak

Quercus gambelii H 10–30 ft (3–9 m)

For the caterpillar (larva) of the Colorado Hairstreak Butterfly to undergo metamorphosis, it must feed on the leaves of the Gambel Oak.

KEY FACTS

The tree has crooked branches.

+ leaves: Alternate, 3–6 in (8–15 cm), yellow-green, broadest beyond middle to uniformly wide; 5–9 lobes; deep sinuses

+ flowers/fruits: Catkins typically oak; acorns to 1 in (2.5 cm), mostly round; caps cover to a third of nut

+ range: Utah, Wyoming, Arizona, New Mexico

A tall shrub or small tree, the Gambel Oak (White Oak group) is the most common deciduous oak in most of the Rocky Mountains, widespread and abundant in the foothills and lower elevations on dry slopes and in canyons. The slopes can be covered in clonal thickets of the tree, the result of sprouting from tuber-like parts of the root system. Farther south, it exists in mixed stands. The tree's small size prevents the fine wood from being commercially significant, but it is used for fires and to make fence posts. Deer and livestock browse the foliage, and acorns provide food for turkeys and squirrels, as well as domestic stock.

Oregon White Oak/Garry Oak

Quercus garryana H to 50 ft (15 m)

The only oak native to British Columbia, Washington, and northern Oregon, the Oregon White Oak is the most commercially important oak in the West.

KEY FACTS

The tree often bears mistletoe.

+ leaves: Alternate, 3–4 in (8–10 cm), broadest beyond middle to uniformly wide; 5–9 lobes; teeth variable, sinuses deep

+ flowers/fruits: Catkins typically oak; acorns to 1.5 in (3.8 cm); caps cover to a third of nut

+ range: Central California to southwestern British Columbia

The Oregon White Oak is a shrub to medium-size tree with a dense, spreading crown. It exists in pure stands or mixed with other hardwoods or conifers. Its ecological foes include fire suppression. Natural grass fires did not harm the oaks but burned out young Douglas-firs beneath them. In the absence of fires, the Douglas-firs become established, and the oaks cannot survive in their shade. Other threats are development and invasive nonnatives. In Oregon White Oak woods in British Columbia, more than 80 percent of the understory is nonnative, and in Oak Bay on Vancouver Island, a permit is required to cut even a branch from established trees.

Shingle Oak
Quercus imbricaria H to 65 ft (20 m)

A stately, medium-size tree, the Shingle Oak is planted for shade or as a windbreak, a hedge, an ornamental, or a street tree. It is our most cold-hardy oak.

KEY FACTS

The lower branches may droop.

+ **leaves:** Alternate, 4–6 in (10–15 cm), oval, unlobed, broadly pointed, with one bristle; margins somewhat wavy; yellow-brown to russet in fall

+ **flowers/fruits:** Catkins typically oak; acorns to 0.7 in (1.8 cm); caps cover about half of nut

+ **range:** Midwest and upper South

The Shingle Oak (a member of the Red Oak group; see Northern Red Oak, p. 98) is never a dominant species in a mixed woods, probably because of its intolerance of shade. It is not a commercially important timber tree, although one of its main practical uses gives it its common name. The wood is pale reddish brown, heavy, hard, and coarse grained, and is used to make split shingles. This use is probably related as well to its scientific name, *imbricaria*, derived from the Latin word for "tile." It also may refer to the overlapping scales of the winter bud. The acorns are especially bitter.

Valley Oak/California White Oak

Quercus lobata H to 82 ft (25 m)

The largest oak tree in the United States and Canada is a Valley Oak in California's Round Valley called the Henley Oak, which is 151 feet (46 m) tall and more than 500 years old.

KEY FACTS

The twigs often weep; salt in the air makes the tree scrubby to 4 mi (6.4 km) inland.

+ **leaves:** Alternate, to 4 in (10 cm); 9–11 deep, rounded lobes

+ **flowers/fruits:** Catkins typically oak; acorns 1.2–2.5 in (3–5.6 cm), narrow, acutely conical or bullet-shaped; caps covering nut base

+ **range:** Endemic to California

A California icon, the Valley Oak (White Oak group) is a tree of valleys in the state's inner and middle coastal ranges. When English explorer George Vancouver visited the Santa Clara Valley in 1792, the expanses of Valley Oak savanna reminded him of a closely planted stand with the understory removed, and he called the trees the "stately lords of the forest." More than 90 percent of the Valley Oak stands were gone by World War II—victims of orchard and vineyard agriculture. The San Francisco Estuary Institute is investigating "re-oaking," hoping to reintegrate Valley Oaks and other natives into California's highly developed landscape.

Overcup Oak

Quercus lyrata H to 65 ft (20 m)

The Overcup Oak's scientific name refers to the overall shape of the leaf, which is said to recall the outline of a lyre. Slow to seed, trees only begin producing seeds at 25 to 30 years of age.

KEY FACTS

The tree has a short trunk.

+ leaves: Alternate, 6–10 in (15–25 cm); 5–9 lobes, irregular, outer pair often making cross shape; deep sinuses

+ flowers/fruits: Catkins typically oak; acorns about 1 in (2.5 cm), round, often almost covered by cap; very long stalk

+ range: Deep South and Mississippi Valley

The Overcup Oak (White Oak group) is a slow-growing, small to medium-size tree of the warm, humid Southeast. Also called Swamp Post Oak, it grows among the Baldcypress and Water Tupelo common in many southern swamps. Its wood warps easily and is generally inferior to that of most of the White Oak group; nonetheless, it is marketed as White Oak and used for general construction and barrels. The Overcup Oak is planted to enhance land for wildlife, and its acorns are eaten by deer, turkeys, and squirrels; ducks also eat the acorns, though because these nuts are so large, they are less useful than those of other oaks.

Bur Oak/Mossycup Oak

Quercus macrocarpa H to 98 ft (30 m)

The Bur Oak has the largest acorn of all our oaks, and its scientific name reflects that: *Macrocarpa* means "big seed." It is a hearty pioneer species with a large native range.

KEY FACTS

The bark forms rectangular blocks.

+ **leaves:** Alternate, to 12 in (30 cm); widest beyond middle; 5–9 lobes; deep sinuses

+ **flowers/fruits:** Catkins typically oak; acorns to 2 in (5 cm); caps cover three-quarters of nut, with mossy or bur-like fringe

+ **range:** Midwest and eastern U.S., south-central Canada

A medium-size to large, spreading tree, the Bur Oak (White Oak group) is cold tolerant and, because of its long tap-root, drought resistant. Its large acorns are important forage for wildlife, including black bears. It is planted as an ornamental and is the most forgiving White Oak of the urban environment. The Bur Oak savannas of the eastern prairie were vital to settlers, providing wood and grazing land. In the early 1900s, these savannas covered 32 million acres. By 1985, as a result of development, including agriculture, and fire suppression, high-quality savanna had declined to 6,400 acres (2,592 ha)—a loss of more than 99 percent.

III

Cherrybark Oak/Swamp Red Oak
Quercus pagoda H to 130 ft (40 m)

The acorns of the Cherrybark Oak provide food for domestic hogs and for wildlife, including larger birds and a number of mammals.

KEY FACTS

The leaf shape recalls a pagoda (thus its scientific name).

+ leaves: Alternate, 5–8 in (13–20 cm), broadest at base; 7–11 lobes, regularly shaped

+ flowers/fruits: Catkins typically oak; acorns 0.6 in (1.6 cm); caps cover a third to half of nut

+ range: Southeastern United States, Mississippi Valley

One of the largest oaks in the South, the Cherrybark Oak (Red Oak group; see Northern Red Oak, p. 98) is similar to the Southern Red Oak, of which it was formerly considered a botanical variety. It prefers moist areas, in riverbanks and in floodplains, especially in the Coastal Plain. The bark recalls that of the Black Cherry, smooth, with flaky ridges, and with a red tint. The trunk is straight, with relatively few limbs, and the wood is strong, making this a good source of timber. The light red-brown wood is heavy, hard, and coarse grained and is used in fine work, including interiors, furniture, cabinets, and floors.

Pin Oak

Quercus palustris H to 82 ft (25 m)

"Pin Oak" is said to refer to persisting dead branches that resemble pins driven into the tree's trunk; another theory is that its branches were used as dowels, or "pins," in barn construction.

KEY FACTS

The tree's interior is dense.

+ leaves: Alternate, to 6 in (15 cm), broadest beyond middle; 5–9 lobes, bristle-tipped; very deep sinuses

+ flowers/fruits: Catkins typically oak; acorns round, with short beak at tip; caps cover only nut base

+ range: Mid-Atlantic and central states and extreme southern Ontario

The fast-growing Pin Oak (Red Oak group; see Northern Red Oak, p. 98) thrives in wet, soggy floodplains and flatlands and tolerates some flooding, but it also inhabits some well-drained and upland areas. The branches spread in age, and the lower ones often droop toward the ground. The wood is weaker than that of the Red Oak and is used in general building, as posts, and for fuel. The Pin Oak is planted extensively as an ornamental and shade tree (even in parts of Australia and Argentina), and cultivars have been developed. Birds that eat its acorns include mallards, wood ducks, blue jays, turkeys, and woodpeckers.

Willow Oak

Quercus phellos H to 98 ft (30 m)

The Willow Oak is so named because its leaves, narrow and tapering at both base and tip, recall the leaves of willows. It is not, however, related to the willows.

KEY FACTS

The leaves are borne stiffly on the twigs.

+ leaves: Alternate, to 5 in (13 cm), tipped by tiny awn; unlobed

+ flowers/fruits: Catkins typically oak; broadly rounded acorns, to 0.5 in (1.3 cm); caps cover a third of thin, saucer-like nut

+ range: Atlantic and Gulf Coastal Plains, Mississippi Valley

The Willow Oak (Red Oak group; see Northern Red Oak, p. 98) inhabits bottomlands and drier areas and is often planted in landscapes and on streets. It consistently has good acorn crops and is important to wildlife. While acorns feed larger animals, the trees host thousands of insect species, few of them pests. For many butterflies and moths, an egg-laying stopover on an oak (for some, a particular species) is required. The larvae need oak leaves to eat, or they cannot metamorphose into adults. Leafhoppers, wasps, and beetles also use oaks, and all these insects provide food for birds and other animals.

Northern Red Oak

Quercus rubra H to 98 ft (30 m)

One of our top timber trees, the Northern Red Oak produces hard, strong, coarse-grained wood, often used in interiors. It is widely planted in Europe for such purposes.

KEY FACTS

The dark gray-brown bark is ridged.

+ **leaves:** Alternate, 4–9 in (10–23 cm), often widest beyond middle; 7–9 lobes; sinuses rounded half-way to midrib

+ **flowers/fruits:** Catkins typically oak; acorns to 1 in (2.5 cm); caps cover a quarter of saucerlike nut

+ **range:** Extreme southeastern Canada, eastern U.S.

The attractive and moderately fast-growing Northern Red Oak is the banner tree of the Red Oak group, which also includes Black Oaks. These oaks' acorns mature in two years, on the previous year's branches. The husk is thin, clinging, and papery, and woolly on the inside. The acorn meat is typically very bitter due to the high levels of tannins, which had to be leached out before native peoples could use them as food. The leaf lobes are often toothed and bear bristles at their tip. The bark is dark, and the texture varies. Species of the Red Oak group will hybridize with one another.

|||||||||||||||||||||||||||||||||||||||||||||||||||||||||||||||||||||||||||||||||||

Shumard Oak

Quercus shumardii H to 115 ft (35 m)

A large, stately southern oak, the Shumard Oak is long lived, and grows relatively quickly. The crown opens with age and the trunk is buttressed in older trees.

KEY FACTS

This deep-rooted oak is often planted near paved areas.

+ leaves: Alternate, to 8 in (20 cm), broad; 5–9 paired lobes; tips toothed, bristled; sinuses deep

+ flowers/fruits: Catkins typically oak; acorns broadly ovate, to 1 in (2.5 cm); caps cover a third of nut

+ range: Eastern, central United States, southwestern Ontario

Acorns of the Shumard Oak (Red Oak group) feed many wildlife species. Humans, too, ate acorns, and there is now renewed interest in the nuts' dietary potential. But acorns, especially in the Red Oak group, contain bitter tannins, which make unprocessed acorns inedible. The Menominee in Wisconsin removed the tannins in a process that was probably not unique to them. They toasted the acorns and removed the husks. They then boiled the acorns in water, which was discarded. They boiled them again, adding alkaline wood ash to accelerate leaching. A final boil removed the ash. The processed acorns were dried and ground into meal or stored.

Post Oak
Quercus stellata H to 65 ft (20 m)

Not a very important timber species, the Post Oak does produce lumber, sold as White Oak, that is used in railroad ties and flooring and, of course, for fence posts.

KEY FACTS

The trunk is gray to light red-brown, becoming ridged.

+ leaves: Alternate, oblong, to 6 in (15 cm); 5 lobes, the center 2 largest, lending a cross-like shape

+ flowers/fruits: Catkins typically oak; acorns to 1 in (2.5 cm); caps cover half of nut, not fringed

+ range: Eastern and central U.S.

Identification of the Post Oak (White Oak group) is difficult because it varies in plant habit, leaf shape, and bark; aberrant populations have been incorrectly designated as a separate species. A character sometimes deemed certain for identification is its cross-shaped leaf, created by two main lobes, which are square and large and project opposite each other from the leaf axis. But other species can have the same arrangement. A better way, though a bit technical, involves use of a hand lens to examine the twigs and the underside of the leaves for stellate hairs, which resemble tufts branching in a starlike (stellate) pattern.

Black Oak

Quercus velutina H to 82 ft (25 m)

The bark of the Black Oak is so rich in tannins that their extraction was once a commercial pursuit. Tannins, used to tan leather, are now synthesized.

KEY FACTS

The bark is gray-black, in vertical plates.

+ **leaves:** Alternate, to 10 in (25 cm); 5–9 lobes, pointed, bristle-tipped; sinuses deep, U-shaped

+ **flowers/fruits:** Catkins typically oak; acorns 0.5 to 0.75 in (1–2 cm); caps cover half of nut

+ **range:** Extreme southwestern Ontario, eastern and central U.S.

The Black Oak (Red Oak group) is common in dry, upland deciduous forests, as well as in savannas, where the eastern forests cede to the prairie. Oak flowers are similar among species, unisexual, and borne on separate catkins, which appear on the same tree before or with the leaves. They usually go unnoticed until they fall onto side-walks and cars. The male catkins are yellow to greenish, long, lax, and pendulous, bear-ing many flowers that make pollen. The stiffer, smaller female catkins bear one to several cupules, each of which contains a flower and will become an acorn cap. Oaks, like most trees bearing catkins, are wind pollinated.

Live Oak

Quercus virginiana H to 115 ft (35 m)

The young U.S. Navy bought extensive Live Oak stands for the use of its shipbuilders. The strong, curved limbs were ideal for fashioning the ships' ribs and other supports.

KEY FACTS

The trunk becomes buttressed with age.

+ leaves: Nearly ever-green, alternate, to 5 in (12 cm); oblong, widest beyond middle, stiff, waxy; sometimes toothed, sometimes curled under

+ flowers/fruits: Catkins typically oak; acorns long, slim; caps scaly, deep

+ range: Coastal Plain from Virginia to Texas

The long-lived and fast-growing Live Oak (White Oak group) has been described, without exaggeration, as majestic, noble, and picturesque. The tree is wide spreading with an extensive, rounded crown. Its massive branches can sprawl so far from the trunk that they bend to touch the ground, sometimes even curving up again. The dark gray bark recalls an alligator's skin. Spanish Moss, which often graces its limbs, completes the picture of this icon of the Deep South. The Live Oak can also be shrubby, and it sprouts vigorously from stumps. Native peoples extracted an oil similar to olive oil from its slim acorns.

Ocotillo/Coach Whip

Fouquieria splendens H to 25 ft (7.6 m)

The Ocotillo is unique and unmistakable. As many as 100 unbranching, whiplike canes grow from the root crown, all angling out slightly for a narrow, vaselike outline.

KEY FACTS

Spiny canes arise from the root crown.

+ **leaves:** Alternate, 2 in (5 cm), oval, fleshy, in bunches

+ **flowers/fruits:** Flowers perfect, scarlet, tubular, clustered at stem tips; fruit capsules with winged seeds

+ **range:** Southern tip of Nevada through Mojave and Sonoran Deserts from California to Arizona

The Ocotillo is called drought deciduous, but it is fairer to say that it leafs out after a rain several times a year. When leafless, the tortuous, gray-green canes handle the photosynthesis. The shrub is even more striking when flowering, the tips of the stems bearing bright red flowers that attract hummingbirds and bees, which pollinate them. *Ocotillo* means "little ocoto," the ocoto being the Montezuma Pine, *Pinus montezumae,* of Mexico and Central America. But the plants don't look alike; they are both just extremely resinous. The stems of the Ocotillo are sometimes removed at the root, and then sunk in the ground to make a living fence.

Witch Hazel
Hamamelis virginiana H to 20 ft (6 m)

Cutting a Y-shaped twig from a Witch Hazel is the first step in making a dowsing rod (several other species are also favored), which "water witches" use to locate, or dowse, water.

KEY FACTS

The Witch Hazel flowers in the fall.

+ **leaves:** Alternate; somewhat scalloped; base rounded to wedge shaped; yellow in fall

+ **flowers/fruits:** Flowers perfect, small but showy, 4 petals, narrow, curly, spreading ribbonlike; fruit capsules 2-beaked, becoming woody

+ **range:** Eastern U.S., Nova Scotia

The Witch Hazel is a shrub or small tree, common in the understory of many eastern woods. The biggest specimens are seen in the mountains of the Carolinas. It has upright branches and an irregular crown, often leaning strongly. Its wood and fruits are of minor value, but it has been used medicinally for centuries. The native peoples boiled many parts of the tree, then used the astringent liquid to treat inflammations. Settlers followed suit, and commercial production eventually began and continues today. Witch Hazel is used as an aftershave lotion, as an eyewash, to treat insect bites, and to soothe hemorrhoids, and may act as a UV protectant.

Sweetgum

Liquidambar styraciflua H to 150 ft (47 m)

Many people may decry the spiny gumballs the Sweetgum produces, but it is widely cultivated for its attractively shaped leaves and its brilliant red, yellow, and orange fall foliage.

KEY FACTS

Maple-like, but the leaves are alternate (opposite in maples) and star shaped.

+ leaves: 5 lobes, pointed, deep, wide

+ flowers/fruits: Flowers in unisexual clusters on same tree; fruits spiky balls, to 1.5 in (3.8 cm)

+ range: Southeast, to Mississippi and Ohio Valleys and on the coast to New York

A medium-size to large tree, the Sweetgum is one of the most common hardwoods in the eastern United States, and one of the most commercially important, second only to the oaks in production. The wood, marketed as satin walnut, takes a finish well and is used in furniture, plywood, cigar boxes, barrels, and pulp. Many cultivars have been developed. The genus name refers to a juice that oozes from the bark, a balsam similar to turpentine, which is extracted from the bark by boiling and made into resin. The juice also will dry on the tree, and dried bits were picked off and used as chewing gum by Native Americans.

Black Walnut

Juglans nigra H to 125 ft (38 m)

The Black Walnut is allelopathic, that is, most plants cannot grow beneath it. It produces a compound, juglone, that inhibits metabolism in many plant species.

KEY FACTS

The trunk is often straight for half its height.

+ leaves: Alternate, compound, to 2 ft (0.6 m); 15–23 leaflets.

+ flowers/fruits: Male flowers in catkins, female on new growth, on same tree; fruits single or paired; husk thick, green; nut black, grooved

+ range: Eastern U.S., southern Ontario

The Black Walnut was once so common that furniture was solid walnut, a beautifully grained, brownish wood. The large walnuts are gone, and the wood is used in gun stocks and some furniture and cabinets. Most walnut furniture is only walnut veneer. Walnuts for ice cream, candy, and cakes support a commercial harvest. These nuts have a stronger, richer flavor than English walnuts, but extracting the meat is real work. The hull is thick and hard, and the interior is a catacomb from which bits must be removed with a nut pick. Anyone trying to remove a nut from its husk will soon have brown fingers: No surprise that dyes and inks are made from the husks.

Bitternut Hickory

Carya cordiformis H to 115 ft (35 m)

The Bitternut Hickory is so named because the nuts are too bitter to eat—even for squirrels. But colonists extracted their oil to burn in lamps, and the husks yield a yellow-brown dye.

KEY FACTS

Leaf buds are yellow.

+ leaves: Alternate, compound, to 8 in (20 cm); 7–11 leaflets

+ flowers/fruits: Male flowers in catkins, female 1 or 2 on spikes, on same tree; fruits clustered, husk thin, opening along winged sutures; nut shell bony, tip sharp

+ range: Eastern U.S., southern Ontario and Quebec

The Bitternut Hickory is one of the largest hickories and the most abundant, found in a range of soil conditions and temperatures. Despite its bitter nuts, it is nonetheless important to our palates, though indirectly. Pecans are grafted onto the rootstock of this wide-ranging hickory so that pecans can be produced north of the Pecan tree's usual, rather southerly range. The Bitternut's dense, strong wood is used in furniture, tool handles, ladders, in woodworking, pulp, and as fuel. Native peoples made bows from the wood and used it in making birch-bark canoes. As with other hickory woods, it is used for smoking meat and to make charcoal.

Pignut Hickory

Carya glabra H 82–132 ft (25–40 m)

The Pignut Hickory, it is thought, got its common name from colonists who noticed that their free-range pigs, rooting in the woods for tree nuts, were especially fond of those of this species.

KEY FACTS

The bark is ridged but not shaggy.

+ leaves: Alternate, compound, to 10 in (25 cm), smooth; 5–7 leaflets

+ flowers/fruits: Male flowers in catkins, female few, in clusters, on same tree; fruits pear-shaped, husk thin, splitting partly; nut unwinged; unribbed

+ range: Eastern U.S., southwestern Ontario

A slow-growing, short-branched, medium-size tree, the Pignut Hickory is the most common hickory in the Appalachians and an important species in oak–hickory forests of the East. The nuts make up as much as 25 percent of the diet of squirrels and are important food items for chipmunks, raccoons, crows, and wood ducks. But for the record, the fruit of a hickory is not a nut but a drupe: Fleshy tissue surrounds a pit, which contains the seed. In the hickories, the fleshy tissue is the husk, the pit is the nut, and the seed is the nut meat. A peach is constructed in much the same way.

Pecan

Carya illinoinensis H 70–100 ft (21–30 m)

The word "pecan" is descended from an Algonquian word, *pakan,* which meant a nut so hard that it had to be cracked with a rock. The word is similar in other native languages.

KEY FACTS

Huge limbs support an oval crown.

+ leaves: Alternate, compound, 12–20 in (30–51 cm); 9–15 leaflets

+ flowers/fruits: Male flowers in catkins, female 1 to few on spike, on same tree; clustered; fruits thin-husked; nut to 2 in (5 cm); shell thin, brown, often with black

+ range: Centered in lower Mississippi Valley.

It is hard to imagine anyone in the world who is not acquainted with the pecan, the soul of pralines, used in ice creams, salads, and scones, and more recently encrusting everything from salmon to seitan. Pecan trees, the largest hickory, are grown far and wide. Spanish and Portuguese explorers took the first trees to Europe in the 16th century. Nevertheless, the United States still supplies about 80 percent of the world's demand. Total U.S. production reached 303 million pounds (137 million kg) in 2012. The long-lived Pecan is also appreciated for its shade, and many cultivars are grown extensively in North America and abroad.

Big Shellbark Hickory/King Nut Hickory
Carya laciniosa H 60–80 ft (18–24 m)

The Big Shellbark Hickory is also called the King Nut Hickory, and deservedly so, because its fruit can be as big as 2.5 inches (6.5 cm) across—just slightly smaller than a tennis ball.

KEY FACTS

The twigs are orange.

+ **leaves:** Alternate, compound, to 24 in (61 cm); 7 leaflets

+ **flowers/fruits:** Male flowers in catkins, female in clusters, on same tree; fruit to 2.5 in (6.5 cm); husk splitting to base; nut large, flattened; shell hard, thick

+ **range:** Midwest, Ohio and upper Mississippi Valleys

The Big Shellbark Hickory is very slow growing, and its fruits are so large that dispersal is hampered; thus, it has never been common. The medium to large tree grows mostly in mixed stands, especially on floodplains and in river swamps. Its nuts are prized for their flavor. The species name, *laciniosa*, from the Latin for "flap," means "shaggy," and the Big Shellbark is similar to the Shagbark Hickory. Key differences distinguish them. The Big Shellbark's bark curls up in strips, though less than the Shagbark's; its leaves have 7 (vs. 5) leaflets, the leaflets have no hairs at the tip of the teeth, the husk of the fruit is thicker, and it prefers wetter habitats.

Shagbark Hickory

Carya ovata H to 150 ft (46 m)

Hickory bark syrup is made from shed Shagbark bark by oven-toasting the bark, then boiling, reducing the liquid's volume, and adding sugar. It is used on meats, in drinks, and on pancakes.

KEY FACTS

Bark on older trees is shaggy.

+ leaves: Alternate, compound, to 14 in (36 cm); 5 leaflets

+ flowers/fruits: Male flowers in catkins, female on short spike, on same tree; fruit to 1.6 in (4 cm); nut usually ridged, shell thick, meat sweet

+ range: Most of eastern U.S., southern Ontario and Quebec

The Shagbark Hickory is similar to the big shellbark but usually has 5 (vs. 7) leaflets, and the leaves have hairs at the tooth tips. The bark is in long, loose plates that curve out, shaggier than in the Big Shellbark. Shagbark nuts are the best of the hickory nuts and were a staple in the diet of native peoples in the tree's range. A food prepared from Shagbark nuts was called *pawcohiccora* in an Algonquian language and altered by settlers to "hickory." Pawcohiccora was a sort of nut milk made from nut meal added to boiling water, and the resulting rich, oily gruel was collected for use in breads and stews.

Mockernut Hickory

Carya tomentosa H to 100 ft (30 m)

The name "Mockernut Hickory" suggests that the nut directs ridicule at the would-be nut eater who, having finally cracked its extremely thick shell, is rewarded by just a small kernel of meat.

KEY FACTS

The bark is not shaggy.

+ leaves: Alternate, compound, 9–14 in (23–36 cm); 5–9 leaflets, toothed, hairy beneath

+ flowers/fruits: Male flowers in catkins, female 2–5 in short spike, on same tree; fruit to 2 in (5 cm); nut 4-angled with pointed tip

+ range: Southern Ontario, most of eastern U.S.

The slow-growing, tall, straight Mockernut is the most common hickory in the South, and it is a key species in oak–hickory forests of the East. Its wood is among the best of the hickories, used to make tool handles, wood splints, furniture, and charcoal. The species label *tomentosa* refers to the hairiness of the underside of the spicy-smelling leaves. The nut meat, though there is not much of it, is sweet, and competition for the nuts from birds and wild mammals is strong. Many cavity dwellers inhabit the tree, including woodpeckers, chickadees, and Black Rat Snakes.

||||||||||||||||||||||||||||||||||||||||||||||||||||||||||||||||||||||||||||||||||

Sassafras

Sassafras albidum H 32–60 ft (10–18 m)

Safrole, which makes Sassafras aromatic, is used to manufacture the drug ecstasy. Sassafras is not a good source, but an Asian relative is, and safrole is illegal in Canada and the United States.

KEY FACTS

The roots and bark smell spicy.

+ leaves: Alternate, simple, to 7 in (18 cm); 0, 2, or 3 lobes

+ flowers/fruits: Male, female flowers on different trees, yellow-green, small, showy in clusters on bare tree; fruit a berrylike drupe, blue, on red stalk

+ range: Eastern U.S., Ontario

Sassafras is planted for its fragrance and for its foliage, which turns yellow to red in the fall. All parts are aromatic. The bark of the root was used to make a tea and to perfume soaps; the shoots were used to make root beer. But the aromatic element, safrole, turned out to be carcinogenic, and these products are now artificially flavored. The Choctaw, native from Florida to Louisiana, have long dried the mucilaginous leaves and ground them to a powder for flavoring and thickening dishes. Named *filé* by French-speaking settlers, the powder is used in Creole and Cajun kitchens to thicken gumbo, soups, and gravy. The leaves are safrole-free.

Northern Spicebush
Lindera benzoin H 6–12 ft (1.8–3.7 m)

The species label *benzoin* refers to the spicy, fragrant leaves, recalling benzoin, a resin obtained from unrelated plants and used in incense (devoid of the compound also called benzoin).

KEY FACTS

The shrub often has several stems.

+ **leaves:** Alternate, simple, entire, 3–6 in (7.6–15 cm), oval, aromatic

+ **flowers/fruits:** Male, female flowers on different trees, yellow, showy in clusters on bare tree; fruit a red, spicy berrylike drupe

+ **range:** Texas, Oklahoma, eastern U.S., southern Ontario

The flowers of the Spicebush are among the first to appear in the spring before the trees leaf out. Though small, the flowers are spectacular if there are enough of this small, graceful tree in the understory. The common name derives from its fruit, which, dried and ground, is used like allspice. The fruit, leaves, and twigs are made into an herbal tea. The Spicebush is the main host (the related Sassafras is another) of the Spicebush Swallowtail, a butterfly that lays its eggs on the plant, in whose foliage the eventual caterpillars will undergo metamorphosis. Spicebush is also a host of the Eastern Tiger Swallowtail.

California Laurel/Oregon Myrtle

Umbellularia californica H 23-100 ft (7-30 m)

When the bank in North Bend, Oregon, closed in 1933, coins worth up to $10 were made of myrtlewood, letting commerce continue. The coins are still accepted but most are in collections.

KEY FACTS

Plant is shrubby in exposed situations.

+ leaves: Evergreen, alternate, to 4 in (10 cm), lance shaped

+ flowers/fruits: Flowers perfect, to 0.6 in (1.4 cm), yellow, in umbrella-like clusters (thus the genus name); fruit a berry, to 1 in (2.5 cm), ripening to purplish

+ range: Southern California to Oregon

The California Laurel is an attractive, medium-size tree with a short trunk that soon divides. This is the only species in the genus, but it has many common names, including California Bay. Its peppery leaves (it is also called Pepperwood) are used as the familiar bay leaf, but they have a stronger flavor. For native tribes, this plant treated many maladies, including headaches, though it can also cause headaches and so is called Headache Tree. The olive-like fruit, called the California Bay nut, is like a tiny avocado (the plants are close relatives). It has a relatively large pit surrounded by oily flesh, both of which are eaten.

Tuliptree/Tulip Poplar/Yellow Poplar
Liriodendron tulipifera H 98–165 ft (30–50 m)

Liriodendron derives from the Greek words for "lily" and "tree"; *tulipifera* means "tulip bearing." The Tuliptree is in the Magnolia family, as study of the flower suggests. It is not a poplar.

KEY FACTS

The twigs turn upward.

+ leaves: Alternate, uniquely 4-lobed; yellow in fall

+ flowers/fruits: Flowers perfect, to 3 in (7.6 cm), at branch tips, tulip-like; 3 green sepals; 6 upright petals, yellow-green, orange at base; fruit a cone-like cluster of winged seeds on a stalk

+ range: Eastern U.S.

The majestic Tuliptree is one of our biggest hardwoods, with a single, straight trunk, which is often half bare. Native peoples used the trunks to make dugout canoes. It is an important tree in eastern hardwood forests, especially at lower elevations. The tree is valued for its light, straight-grained wood, used in interior detail, furniture, general construction, plywood, and pulp. Many animals depend on the tree for seeds, browse, sap, or cover, but bees especially avail themselves of this important honey plant: The flowers from one 20-year-old Tuliptree can provide them with nectar sufficient for 4 pounds (1.8 kg) of honey.

Cucumber-tree

Magnolia acuminata H 60–95 ft (20–30 m)

The name "Cucumber-tree" describes the unripe fruit, a composite of many follicles with their developing seeds. When green, this "cone" is shaped much like a cucumber.

KEY FACTS

The bark is furrowed.

+ leaves: Alternate, simple, entire, 6–10 in (15–25 cm), oval, pointed; gold to maroon in fall

+ flowers/fruits: Flowers perfect, to 3 in (7.6 cm) across; 9 yellow tepals, outer 3 bent back; fruit to 3 in (7.6 cm), cone-like; seeds red

+ range: Louisiana to New York, southern Ontario

The Cucumber-tree has a wide distribution, but it is never abundant, usually scattered in the eastern oak–hickory forests. It is most often found in the mountains, and the largest specimens grow in the southern Appalachians. The hardiest magnolia, it is the only one native to Canada, found, but rare, in Ontario. Its slightly fragrant flower is smaller and not as showy as that of other magnolias, and it is the only *Magnolia* species that has yellow sepals. A number of cultivars have been developed. The wood is similar to Tuliptree wood and is sold alongside it. It is used in crates, cabinets, and some paneling.

Southern Magnolia

Magnolia grandiflora H 65–95 ft (20–29 m)

The Southern Magnolia had traveled to England by 1726, via Mark Catesby, an English naturalist who published and illustrated the first book on the flora and fauna of North America.

KEY FACTS

The bark is smooth, gray-brown.

+ **leaves:** Evergreen, alternate, simple, entire, 3–8 in (7.6–20 cm), oval, shiny, stiff, rusty below

+ **flowers/fruits:** Flowers perfect, to 8 in (20 cm) across, showy, fragrant; 6–12 broad, creamy white tepals; fruit compound, dry; seeds red

+ **range:** Coastal Plain, North Carolina to Texas

This small to medium-size tree of the lowlands is botanically and culturally identified with the South, growing largest in moist and well-drained soils and popular as an ornamental far from its native range. More than 100 cultivars have been developed. Other than the seed, the Southern Magnolia is not used much by wildlife, and the wood is of limited importance, but all parts of the tree have yielded compounds of potential pharmaceutical value. The genus name (and that of the family, Magnoliaceae) was assigned by botanist Carl Linnaeus in honor of French botanist Pierre Magnol of Montpellier, who conceived of the family as an organizing unit in plant taxonomy.

Sweetbay

Magnolia virginiana H to 90 ft (27 m)

Sweetbay is often called "tardily deciduous," but it varies from deciduous in its more northern extent to evergreen in its southern. The tree also grows larger in the South.

KEY FACTS

The bark is smooth.

+ **leaves:** Semi-evergreen, alternate, simple, entire, to 6 in (15 cm), blunt-tipped, silvery below

+ **flowers/fruits:** Flowers perfect, showy, fragrant, to 5.5 in (14 cm) across; 9–12 creamy-white tepals; fruit and seeds red

+ **range:** Coastal Plain and Piedmont, eastern U.S.

A graceful, small to medium-size tree, the Sweetbay prefers low elevations and wet, sandy, acid soils. Its foliage and twigs are aromatic, and its flower has a lemony scent. When a breeze catches the foliage, briefly flashing the leaves' silvery white undersides, the tree ripples with light. Primarily southeastern, it ranges north to Massachusetts, where the discovery in 1806 of a Sweetbay swamp in Gloucester caused a stir among botanists. Jacob Bigelow made the find public in 1814 in his *Plants of Boston*, calling it "our only species of this superb genus." The stand is now the focus of an annual "Save the Sweetbay" event in Gloucester.

Chinaberry Tree
Melia azedarach H to 49 ft (15 m)

The fruit of the Chinaberry contains very hard, reddish, five-grooved seeds that were widely used to make rosaries and other beaded objects before the advent of plastics.

KEY FACTS

The clustered fruits are persistent and toxic.

+ **leaves:** Alternate, once or twice compound, to 2.2 in (6 cm); toothed or lobed, smooth leaflets

+ **flowers/fruits:** Perfect, small, fragrant, in loose clusters; 5 petals, lavender, with purple tubular corona; fruit a yellow-brown drupe

+ **range:** Nonnative; widespread

Native to the Himalaya and eastern Asia, the Chinaberry (in the Mahogany family) was brought to South Carolina in the late 1700s as an ornamental and a shade tree. It escaped and is now invasive, especially common in thickets in old fields and on disturbed sites. The Chinaberry is ideally suited for invasion. It is fast growing and short lived, and produces huge numbers of seeds, which are dispersed by birds. Its seedpods persist on the tree into winter; it forms colonies by sprouting; and it is drought tolerant and a soil generalist with essentially no pests. The weak, soft wood has been used in furniture and cabinetry, as well as for firewood.

Osage Orange
Maclura pomifera H 40–60 ft (12–18 m)

A female tree will bear normal-looking fruit even if there is no male nearby to provide pollen; the fruit will not, however, contain seeds. The tree is not an orange but is in the Mulberry family.

KEY FACTS

The bark has an orange cast.

+ leaves: Alternate, simple, to 5 in (13 cm), oval, pointed; leaf axils with 1-in (2.5-cm) spine

+ flowers/fruits: Male, female flowers on separate trees; fruits orange-like, bumpy, to 5 in (10–13 cm) across; skin with milky sap

+ range: South-central U.S.

The Osage Orange is a medium-size tree of rich bottomlands but tolerates a range of conditions. Though of a rather narrow natural range, it has been planted and has naturalized through most of the eastern United States and in Ontario. It is planted in hedges and, because of its spines, was used in cattle "fences" before the advent of barbed wire. The bright orange wood is not commercially important, though it is good firewood. Squirrels may excavate the fruit to eat its seeds, but the tree is not important to wildlife. A large, extinct animal, such as the Mammoth or a horselike mammal, may have been the natural disperser of Osage Orange seeds.

White Mulberry

Morus alba H to 50 ft (15 m)

The fastest known movement in plants is that of a mechanism in the White Mulberry's male flowers that ejects pollen into the air. The structure triggers at more than half the speed of sound.

KEY FACTS

The leaves are usually smooth above.

+ **leaves:** Alternate, oval, to 4 in (10 cm), serrate, often deeply lobed

+ **flowers/fruits:** Male and female catkins on same or different trees; fruit aggregates of drupes, 0.75 in (2 cm), ovoid, red turning white, pink, or purple-black

+ **range:** Eastern U.S. and Ontario

The White Mulberry has been cultivated for several thousand years in China as a host for the silkworm. This spreading tree was introduced to North America for the same purpose, but the attempt failed—by no fault of the trees. They are naturalized across the eastern United States and into Ontario, often seen on roadsides and in abandoned fields. The invasive nonnative also crosses with the native Red Mulberry. Distinguishing the White Mulberry from the Red can be tricky, as the species overlap in leaf shape and hairiness. The White has leaves that are most often glossy above, often curling up.

Red Mulberry

Morus rubra H to 66 ft (20 m)

The inner bark of the young shoots of Red Mulberry was often used to produce fiber cord and cloth for garments. Choctaw women often wore cloaks made of woven fiber cord.

KEY FACTS

The leaves are often rough above.

+ leaves: Alternate, to 5.5 in (14 cm), entire or lobed, rounded and long-pointed

+ flowers/fruits: Male and female catkins on separate trees; fruits aggregates of drupes, 1.2 in (3 cm), cylindrical, red to purple to almost black

+ range: Eastern U.S., southern Ontario

The Red Mulberry is our most common native mulberry. It is also often planted in yards, but in summer the ground under a female tree will be covered with overripe berries, so some people buy only male trees. Those people will not enjoy the berries, which for centuries have been consumed raw and in beverages, preserves, cakes, and dumplings. The fruits are usually used immediately, and are seldom seen for sale because they do not keep for long. Genetic pollution of *Morus rubra* by the nonnative *M. alba*, the White Mulberry, is recognized as a problem. In Canada, the problem is considered serious enough that the Red Mulberry is listed as endangered.

California Wax Myrtle/Pacific Bayberry

Morella californica H to 26 ft (8 m)

Pacific Bayberry fruits are a source of wax and fragrance that have been used to make candles and soap. Dyes were also made from the berries.

KEY FACTS

The leaves are sticky.

+ **leaves:** Evergreen, alternate, to 4 in (10 cm), narrow, broader, sparsely toothed toward tip

+ **flowers/fruits:** Male, female, perfect flowers in catkins on same plant, in various combinations, inconspicuous; fruit a purple drupe with white wax coating

+ **range:** Lower British Columbia south

The aromatic Pacific Bayberry is a shrub or small tree of the coast. It is often planted as an ornamental, for its evergreen foliage, to attract wildlife, to serve as a hedge or screen, or to retard erosion. The roots contain bacteria that fix nitrogen from the air, making it usable as a plant nutrient. In 2007, a leaf blight, an infection by a fungus-like organism that is known also to damage apples and pears, was noted on the Pacific Bayberry in Oregon. The lower plant is affected first, but much of the plant is eventually defoliated. The leaves may regrow, but repeated defoliations could kill affected branches.

Wax Myrtle/Southern Bayberry

Morella cerifera H to 40 ft (12 m)

One of the birds that take cover in and eat the berries of the Wax Myrtle is *Setophaga coronata coronata*—the Myrtle Warbler, named for its association with the shrub.

KEY FACTS

The gray bark can be almost white.

+ leaves: Evergreen, alternate, to 4 in (10 cm), narrow, slightly toothed, broader near tip

+ flowers/fruits: Male and female catkins on separate plants; drupe green with light-blue wax coating, borne on female plants

+ range: Eastern and Gulf Coastal Plains

Alarge, evergreen shrub or small tree, the Wax Myrtle is a coastal plant of sandy to moist soils, often forming thickets. It is widely planted, and cultivars have been developed. *Cerifera* means "wax bearing," and all bayberries have been used to make candles. The berries are boiled and the melted wax skimmed from the surface of the water and molded or dipped to make fragrant candles. *Bayberry* means *"berryberry"*: In this usage, the word "bay" comes from the French *baie*, or "berry." But the word also hints at the leaf's aroma, invoking the bay leaf, a culinary herb for which aromatic Wax Myrtle leaves have long been substituted by native peoples and Europeans to flavor seafood and other dishes.

Tasmanian Bluegum

Eucalyptus globulus H to 263 ft (80 m)

An ingredient of cough drops and chest ointments, aromatic eucalyptus oil from Tasmanian Bluegum also has been used to treat arthritis and in mouthwashes and insect repellents.

KEY FACTS

The bark shreds in long strips.

+ leaves: Evergreen, alternate, to 7.1 in (18 cm), narrow, tapering to a long point, hanging

+ flowers/fruits: Flowers single, in upper leaf axils; 4 petals, fused into a cap that falls from the bud; fruit a woody capsule

+ range: Nonnative in far West

Thousands of acres of Bluegum were planted for timber in California in the late 1800s. A flop wood-wise but still grown as a windbreak or ornamental, it escaped and now thrives north into British Columbia. But Bluegum is most invasive in and poses the greatest threat to California. Its flammable oils and old bark that piles up beneath it make it incendiary. Of the energy behind the 1991 Oakland Hills firestorm, which killed 25 and burned 3,000 homes, 70 percent came from eucalyptus. (More than 100 other "eucs," including the River Redgum, *E. camaldulensis,* and the Forest Redgum, *E. tereticornis,* also grow in California.)

Water Tupelo

Nyssa aquatica H to 115 ft (35 m)

As its common and scientific names suggest, the Water Tupelo often grows in wet places, including Baldcypress and other swamps and periodically flooded areas.

KEY FACTS

Its feet are wet to flooded.

+ leaves: Alternate, simple, to 8.5 in (22 cm), pointed, with few teeth; long stalk

+ flowers/fruits: Male flowers in heads, female solitary, some perfect, on same tree; fruit a purple drupe, 1.5 in (4 cm)

+ range: Virginia to Texas (except peninsular Florida), Mississippi Valley

The Water Tupelo is a long-lived, medium-size to large tree of the Coastal Plain. If it grows in very wet places, the trunk is swollen and buttressed, sometimes hugely so. Above that (or if not buttressed), the trunk is long, straight, and clear, supporting a narrow, open crown. Many fruits are produced, and the seeds are dispersed mainly by water. The fruits are also eaten by wildlife, including songbirds, turkeys, and groundhogs. The wood is weak and soft, used in paneling, boxes, and crates. In addition to its use in pulp, the wood of the swollen base is a preferred medium of wood carvers. Honey from this and other tupelos is prized.

Blackgum/Black Tupelo

Nyssa sylvatica H to 131 ft (40 m)

The trunk of the Black Tupelo is straight, extending to the top of the tree. The leaves are brilliant yellow, red, orange, and purple in the fall. It is cultivated and popular as an ornamental tree.

KEY FACTS

Its feet are dry to moist.

+ **leaves:** Alternate, simple, to 6 in (15 cm), rounded or broadly pointed; stalk short

+ **flowers/fruits:** Male flowers in dense heads, female 2 to several in cluster, some perfect, on same tree; fruit drupe 0.5 in (1.2 cm), usually 3–5, blue

+ **range:** Eastern United States, southern Ontario

The Black Tupelo is a widely distributed, medium-size to large tree of the open woods in uplands and well-drained alluvial bottoms, especially in acidic soils. The tree has dense foliage, and its crown is conic to flat. In old trees, the bark is blocky, resembling the skin of an alligator. Its fruits are eaten by many birds and mammals, and bees collect nectar from its flowers to make the popular tupelo honey. In addition to the usual uses as lumber, veneer, and pulp, Black Tupelo is used to make rollers, bowls, blocks, mallets, gun stocks, wheel hubs, and pistol grips.

White Ash

Fraxinus americana H to 82 ft (25 m)

This tree is called the White Ash because the underside of the leaflets, in contrast to the deep green above, are so light green as to appear white.

KEY FACTS

Its twigs are smooth.

+ leaves: Opposite, compound, to 12 in (30 cm); 5–9 leaflets, to 6 in (15 cm), white-green below; yellow to red to purple in fall

+ flowers/fruits: Unisexual clusters on separate trees; fruit a samara, broadest near tip

+ range: Eastern U.S.; southern Ontario to Cape Breton Island

Our most common native ash, the White Ash is a tree of well-drained, rich soils, usually growing in mixed hardwood stands. It is the most valuable ash for timber, going into furniture and paneling. Also, most baseball bats are made from its wood, as are snowshoes, electric guitar bodies, and lobster pots. All *Fraxinus* species are menaced by the Emerald Ash Borer, a metallic green beetle native to Asia that was first seen in North America in 2002, and has been reported in 18 states as of 2013. The borer destroys a tree's transport system, killing half the branches in a year and most of the crown in two. It has killed 60 million ashes so far.

Green Ash

Fraxinus pennsylvanica H to 66 ft (20 m)

Its broad tolerance for different types and acid levels of soils makes the Green Ash a popular and widely planted ornamental and shade tree, as well as a successful street tree.

KEY FACTS

The leaves are golden in fall.

+ **leaves:** Opposite, compound, to 12 in (30 cm); 7–9 leaflets, to 6 in (15 cm), on narrowly winged stalks

+ **flowers/fruits:** Unisexual clusters on separate trees; fruit a samara, broadest at or above middle

+ **range:** Alberta to Cape Breton, to Texas and northern Florida

The Green Ash is the most widely distributed ash in North America, inhabiting wet uplands, floodplains, and stream banks, growing in mixed-hardwood forests or pure stands. It is most common in the Mississippi Valley. Small to medium-size, it has a tall, slender trunk, and its crown is irregular to rounded. It produces a large seed crop that is important to turkeys, quail, squirrels, and other small mammals. Moose and deer browse on the shoots and leaves. Its pale brown hardwood is used for similar purposes as that of the White Ash, and it, too, is affected by the Emerald Ash Borer.

Empress Tree/Princess Tree/Royal Paulownia

Paulownia tomentosa H to 60 ft (18 m)

Paulownia was named for Anna Pavlovna, queen of the Netherlands, daughter of Emperor Paul I of Russia, and granddaughter of Catherine the Great.

KEY FACTS

The dry pods are persistent.

+ **leaves:** Opposite, to 12 in (30 cm), some-times 3-lobed, hairy above, densely so below; long-pointed; base heart-shaped

+ **flowers/fruits:** Perfect, to 2.5 in (6 cm), tubular, purple, fragrant, in pyramidal clusters to 14 in (35 cm); fruit capsules large

+ **range:** Widely invasive

The Empress Tree, a native of China, has been cultivated in Japan and Europe for several hundred years. It was introduced to North America in 1834 for its appealing clusters of purple flowers. Now naturalized and invasive, and cold hardy as far north as Massachusetts, it is seen planted in gardens and parks, but also in vacant lots where it has seeded itself. Each capsule contains 2,000 seeds; one tree can make 20 million in a crop. For a different vision of how prolific it is, consider that in the 1800s, when porcelain was shipped out of China, instead of excelsior, they packed it in the tiny, fluffy-winged seeds of the Empress Tree.

‖‖

American Sycamore

Platanus occidentalis H 98–130 ft (30–40 m)

English settlers named the tree because its leaves recalled the Sycamore Maple *(Acer pseudoplatanus),* from England. Leaves are similar, but sycamores and maples are not related.

KEY FACTS

The bark falls in plaques.

+ **leaves:** Alternate, simple, 4–8 in (10–20 cm); 3–5 very shallow lobes

+ **flowers/fruits:** Male and female heads on same tree; fruit a narrow achene, with tuft aiding dispersal, in dense sphere from long stem, to 1.4 in (3.5 cm), eventually shattering

+ **range:** Eastern U.S.

The American Sycamore, the most massive tree of eastern North America, can be identified from far away by its thick single trunk, with its distinctive, irregular patches of green, tan, and white resulting from shedding, older bark. Found among hardwoods of the bottomlands in nature, the tree is grown for shade and is planted on city streets. It is sometimes infected with plane anthracnose, which causes leaf dieback and is host to the Eastern Mistletoe. It was under one of these trees on Wall Street that the New York Stock Exchange began in 1792 with 24 parties signing what became known as the Buttonwood Agreement. The Sycamore is also called Buttonwood.

London Plane Tree

Platanus × acerifolia H 66–115 ft (20–35 m)

Half the planted trees in London are the London Plane Tree. First used in England in the mid-1600s, it became *the* tree in the capital because it could withstand the challenges of urban life.

KEY FACTS

Fruiting balls appear threaded.

+ **leaves:** Alternate, simple, 4–8 in (10–20 cm); 3–7 shallow lobes

+ **flowers/fruits:** Male and female heads dense, on same tree; fruit a narrow achene with tuft aiding dispersal, in dense spheres (mostly 2) on stem, eventually shattering

+ **range:** Hybrid; grown widely in North America

The London Plane Tree is easily confused with the American Sycamore, especially because of their similar patchy, multishaded trunks. The leaves and the fruits distinguish the two. This tree is a hybrid between the American Sycamore and the Oriental Plane Tree *(P. orientalis)*. The latter developed resistance to plane anthracnose, a disease from Asia, with which it evolved. Resistance inherited from the Oriental Plane Tree has made the London hybrid popular in eastern North America, where anthracnose has marred many American Sycamores, which have no resistance. But its resistance varies.

California Sycamore
Platanus racemosa H to 115 ft (35 m)

The largest California Sycamores are found in the canyons, though the species also grows on stream banks and in other moist areas in the central and southern areas of the state.

KEY FACTS

The tree often leans.

+ leaves: Alternate, simple, to 10 in (25 cm); 3–5 lobes, half as long as leaf

+ flowers/fruits: Flowers tiny, male and female heads on same tree; fruit a narrow achene, with tuft aiding dispersal, in dense maroon spheres, 2–7 appear to be strung zigzag on a stem

+ range: California

The California Sycamore, native in the foothills and Coast Ranges, is similar to the American Sycamore, but with more strongly lobed leaves. Its bark, too, is shed in plaques, and the trunk is an irregular patchwork of brown, gray, and white, but on older trees, it is furrowed with broad ridges. The species also often has multiple trunks. Native peoples used its larger leaves to wrap baking bread, the inner bark was used medicinally and for food, and the branches were used to build homes. Plane anthracnose can cause leaf dieback, and the tree is a host to the Bigleaf Mistletoe, also known as Sycamore Mistletoe.

California Buckthorn/California Coffeeberry

Rhamnus californica H to 20 ft (6 m)

The California Buckthorn is often called Coffeeberry for its fruit, which progresses from green to red to black, much as the coffee plant's fruit. It does not, however, provide a coffee substitute.

KEY FACTS

This species often has multiple trunks.

+ leaves: Evergreen or nearly so, alternate, simple, to 3 in (7.6 cm), lustrous

+ flowers/fruits: Flowers perfect, small, inconspicuous, star-shaped, greenish, in small clusters in leaf axils; fruit is a berry, 0.5 in (1.3 cm)

+ range: California

The California Buckthorn grows as a shrub or small tree on coastal chaparral, on hillsides, and in ravines. It also occurs in parts of Oregon, Arizona, and New Mexico. The plant flowers and sets seed profusely and so is valuable in erosion control. Horticulturally, it is planted for its colorful berries and their contrast with the foliage. The berries are eaten by goats, deer, black bears, and livestock, as well as birds. They are sweet but laxative; native peoples in the Buckthorn's range used it medicinally for that reason, as well as to soothe toothaches by holding a warmed root against the gum and to treat various skin ailments.

Red Mangrove

Rhizophora mangle H to 82 ft (25 m)

Red Mangrove seeds germinate when still attached to the tree.
Seedlings grow to 12 in (30 cm), resembling hanging pods. They
fall and float until reaching a suitable substrate, then take root.

KEY FACTS

Aerial roots arise from
the stems.

+ leaves: Evergreen,
opposite, simple, to
6 in (15 cm), leathery,
shiny

+ flowers/fruits:
Perfect, to 1 in
(2.5 cm) across, pale
yellow, 2 or 3 at leaf
axils; fruit egg-shaped,
seeds germinating and
seedlings elongating
before falling

+ range: Southern-
most Florida

Some 70 trees and shrubs in more than 20 families are
called mangrove, uniquely adapted to the tropical inter-
tidal zone. Only one, the Rhizophoraceae, is the Mangrove
family, and only one of its species is native to North America,
the Red Mangrove. Its mangrove look is due to its odd seedlings and to its arching aerial roots, which admit oxygen,
often lacking in the stagnant sediments. The
White Mangrove, *Laguncularia racemosa*
(family Combretaceae), inhabiting higher
ground, is also native to Florida. It, too,
has aerial roots and precocious seedlings.
The United Nations estimates that 20
percent of mangrove ecosystems were
lost worldwide from 1980 to 2010.

III

Saskatoon/Pacific Serviceberry

Amelanchier alnifolia H to 40 ft (12 m)

The city of Saskatoon, Saskatchewan, was named after the berry (and not vice versa), in 1882. The word "Saskatoon" comes from a Cree phrase meaning "early berry."

KEY FACTS

Fall leaves are orange to red.

+ **leaves:** Alternate, to 2.4 in (6 cm), oval to round, toothed at tip

+ **flowers/fruits:** Flowers perfect, to 1.2 in (3 cm), fragrant, 3–20 at branch ends; 5 white petals; fruit a blue, sweet berry-like pome, to 0.4 in (1.1 cm).

+ **range:** Alaska to northern California, to Wisconsin, Ontario

The word "Saskatoon" refers to both the berry and the plant. This shrub or small tree often forms thickets by sprouting from its extensive root crown and rhizome network, which makes it useful in erosion control. Twigs, foliage, and bark make the plant important to large game species, such as deer and moose, especially in winter, and the fruits provide food for many birds and mammals, including the black bear. The fruit looks like a blueberry. Native peoples have long eaten them, including in fermented form, and added to pemmican for its flavor and as a preservative. It is raised commercially, and growers market it as a superfruit, like blueberries and acai berries.

Hawthorn

Crataegus species H 16–49 ft (5–15 m)

People born on Manitoulin Island, Ontario, in Lake Huron, call themselves haweaters, because the island is home to many Hawthorns.

KEY FACTS

Fruits recall tiny apples.

+ leaves: Alternate, to 4 in (10 cm), entire, toothed, or lobed, even in same species

+ flowers/fruits: Flowers perfect, to 1 in (2.5 cm) across, single or clustered; 5 petals, white to red; fruit a pome, to 1 in (2.5 cm), yellow, red, or nearly black

+ range: All but northernmost Canadian provinces

While a tree may rather easily be identified as a Hawthorn, determining its species is often difficult. Variation within a species can sometimes be greater than that between two species, and they have a complicated breeding biology. As a result, more than 1,700 names have been published worldwide for what are now believed to represent around 200 species. Here, we are considering the genus only. The thorns are modified branches that can be 3 inches (7.6 cm) long. Densely branched, Hawthorns provide excellent cover and nesting sites for songbirds, and many, especially waxwings and thrushes, eat the fruits, called "haws."

||||||||||||||||||||||||||||||||||||||||||||||||||||||||||||||||||||||||||||||||||||||||||

American Plum
Prunus americana H to 36 ft (11 m)

The American Plum was likely cultivated in the Great Plains before European contact. Its branches figure in the Cheyenne Sun Dance, and the Navajo made a reddish purple dye with the roots.

KEY FACTS

The tree is spiny.

+ leaves: Alternate, to 4 in (10 cm), pointed, tapered at base, finely toothed

+ flowers/fruits: Flowers perfect, to 1 in (2.5 cm) across, clustered 2–5, with 5 white petals; fruit drupe to 1 in (2.5 cm), orange to red

+ range: Eastern and midwestern North America

The American Plum is the most widely ranging wild plum in North America, a tree of mixed hardwood forests and edge habitats. It is probably not native to Canada, but its range has been expanded around the world by cultivation. Like many woody species of the Rose family, this one readily sends up suckers, which makes it valuable in erosion control. Though its small size makes its wood unimportant, its showy, fragrant flowers have made it a popular choice as an ornamental tree in parks and yards, and it is raised in orchards for its fruits, which are made into jellies and pies.

Mexican Plum
Prunus mexicana H to 35 ft (10.6 m)

Although found in northern Mexico, the Mexican Plum is a tree of the south-central U.S. states. It was named in 1882 from a specimen collected in the northeastern Mexican state of Coahuila.

KEY FACTS

The bark is furrowed.

+ **leaves:** Alternate, simple, to 4 in (10 cm), twice fine-toothed, hairy below; hairy stalk

+ **flowers/fruits:** Flowers perfect, to 1 in (2.5 cm) across, clustered 2–4; 5 white petals; fruit drupe, to 1.2 in (3 cm), red to purple

+ **range:** Midwest, south-central states

The Mexican Plum is sometimes confused with the American Plum. The former's hairy leafstalks and larger fruits can help distinguish it. It is common, though usually scattered, in a variety of habitats, including woodland edges and open fields, as well as richer woodlands. It seldom sends up suckers and is mostly single trunked, which makes it useful for grafting cultivated plum varieties. Its branching pattern and dark, peeling bark make it a favorite in bonsai. Though the juicy flesh is tart, it is improved with sugar and is often made into jelly and jam. It is often planted as an ornamental.

Black Cherry
Prunus serotina H to 110 ft (34 m)

The Black Cherry was likely grown as an ornamental in Paris as early as 1630. It spread through Europe and it is now considered a forest pest in Denmark, Germany, and the Netherlands.

KEY FACTS

The bark is plated in age.

+ leaves: Alternate, to 6 in (15 cm), finely blunt-toothed

+ flowers/fruits: Flowers perfect, showy in pendulous spike to 6 in (15 cm); 5 white petals; fruit drupe, to 0.4 in (1 cm), on flower spike, almost black

+ range: East, to Nova Scotia; New Mexico, into Arizona

The Black Cherry is our largest and most widely distributed cherry. A fast-growing pioneer in abandoned fields, it is also found in mixed stands of hardwoods and conifers. Its red-brown wood is hard, polishes well, and rivals walnut for use in cabinetry. Many birds and small animals eat its fruits, as do humans. The small cherries are bitter and so are made into sweet jams, but they are also used in soft drinks and ice cream because their flavor is more intense than that of sweet cherries. The tree is often damaged by tent caterpillars and Japanese beetles. The species label, *serotina,* means "late"; this species blooms after other cherries.

||||||||||||||||||||||||||||||||||||||||||||||||||||||||||||||||||||||||||||||||||||||

Klamath Plum

Prunus subcordata H to 26 ft (8 m)

The first European settlers in Pacific states soon began to cultivate the Klamath Plum, which they considered the region's most useful fruit. It took botanists until the mid-1800s to discover it.

KEY FACTS

The tree is spiny.

+ leaves: Alternate, to 3 in (7.6 cm), almost round; margin once or twice toothed

+ flowers/fruits: Flowers perfect, small, clustered 2–7; petals white or pinkish; fruit drupe, to 1.2 in (3 cm), dark red or yellow, flesh juicy

+ range: Pacific states

The Klamath Plum is the only plum tree native to the Pacific coast, a large, thicket-forming shrub or a small tree growing in pure stands or with other hardwoods or evergreens. It is found on the eastern slopes of the Coastal Ranges and Sierra Nevada of California and in the dry valleys east of the Cascade Mountains of Oregon and Washington. Although the plum is tart, it is eaten both fresh and dried, and a number of cultivars have been developed. The species name, *subcordata,* means that the base of the leaf is almost cordate, or heart shaped. The tree is too small for its wood to have commercial value.

Chokecherry

Prunus virginiana H to 26 ft (8 m)

Chokecherry fruit is unappealing (thus the common name) but is used in jellies, pies, and wine. Some cultivars have nonbitter fruit, and researchers hope to improve the species as a food plant.

KEY FACTS

The fruit is astringent.

+ **leaves:** Alternate, to 4 in (10 cm); finely, sharply toothed

+ **flowers/fruits:** Flowers in loose clusters to 6 in (15 cm), fragrant, 5 white petals; fruit drupe, to 0.4 in (1 cm), red or purple, thick-skinned, juicy

+ **range:** British Columbia to Newfoundland, northern U.S.

Native peoples used the Chokecherry to treat many ailments; the U.S. Pharmacopeia listed the bark as recently as 1970. The very nutritious fruits have always been eaten, appearing in stews, in pemmican, or alongside salmon. Some people believe that the Chokecherry holds more promise even than the Saskatoon for large-scale culture because of the cherry's hardiness and fruit yield. At present, Chokecherries come from wild trees, and not even 5 percent are harvested. The Chokecherry became North Dakota's state fruit, because archaeologists have found its pits at many sites there. Birds are so fond of the fruit that the tree is sometimes called the Virginia Bird Cherry.

Black Cottonwood

Populus trichocarpa H to 164 ft (50 m)

The Black Cottonwood is the first woody species to have had its genome mapped. It was important to map all the genes of a tree because of wood's economic importance.

KEY FACTS

The trunk is clean.

+ **leaves:** Alternate, to 4 in (10 cm), pointed, finely toothed; leafstalk not flat

+ **flowers/fruits:** Male catkins dense, to 2 in (5 cm), female loose, to 3 in (7.6 cm), on separate trees; fruit capsule 3-parted, to 0.5 in (1.3 cm)

+ **range:** Alaska through California, Idaho

The Black Cottonwood is the largest hardwood in the West and our biggest poplar. This majestic tree is especially successful on deep, rich soils built up by river silting, often developing pure stands. It also grows alongside other hardwoods and conifers. The capsule fruits of cottonwoods develop in the pendent female catkin, appearing as though attached to a thread. The seeds are tiny and bear cottony tufts that aid in their dispersal and that give the trees their name. Native tribes used the inner bark medicinally. It contains salicin, a compound related to aspirin that can reduce inflammation and break a fever.

Eastern Cottonwood

Populus deltoides ssp. *deltoides* H 72–100 ft (22–30 m)

The common name refers to the fluffy-tufted seeds. Another name is Necklace Poplar, a reference to the female catkin's bearing mature fruits and resembling a strand of beads.

KEY FACTS

The trunk branches are massive.

+ leaves: Alternate, simple, to 7 in (17.8 cm), triangular, tapering to tip; margin toothed, wavy; leafstalk slender, flat

+ flowers/fruits: Male and female catkins to 3 in (7.6 cm), on different trees; fruit capsule, to 0.5 in (1.3 cm), in 3–4 parts

+ range: Eastern U.S.

The Eastern Cottonwood is a tall tree of moist, rich lowland forests and is therefore largely absent from the higher Appalachians. The trunk soon branches, creating a wide, spreading crown, and the upright limbs arch at their ends for a vaselike form. The Eastern Cottonwood is often planted for quick shade, but any planting should be well thought out because the extensive roots can invade pipes and buckle sidewalks. Many people plant the male tree, which does not produce cotton. The species label, *deltoides*, refers to the triangular shape of the leaf. The flattened and extra-flexible leaf stem makes the leaf shake in even a calm breeze.

Plains Cottonwood
Populus deltoides ssp. *monilifera* H to 88 ft (27 m)

Isolated populations west of the Rocky Mountains in the Pacific Northwest were recently determined to be the Plains Cottonwood, previously believed to grow only east of the Rockies.

KEY FACTS

This is the largest tree of the Plains.

+ leaves: Alternate, to 3.5 in (8.9 cm); tapering to pointed tip; margin coarsely toothed, wavy; leaf-stalk slender, flat

+ flowers/fruits: Male and female catkins on different trees; fruit capsule, to 0.4 in (1.1 cm), conical

+ range: Manitoba to Texas Panhandle

The Plains Cottonwood has been considered a separate species, *P. sargentii,* but it is now usually thought of as a subspecies of *P. deltoides;* the subspecies has smaller leaves that have fewer teeth. It is the largest tree and the most abundant cottonwood of the Great Plains, found in pure stands in rich riverside habitats but otherwise mixed with other hardwoods. As in most catkin-bearing trees, cottonwood catkins form before the trees leaf out, the hallmark of pollination by wind. The Dakota ate the inner bark of the spring sprouts and also fed them to their horses. The subspecific label, *monilifera,* means "resembling a string of beads."

III

Quaking Aspen
Populus tremuloides H 39–60 ft (12–18 m)

A recent study tested the Quaking Aspen's odd, characteristic movement. Stems were splinted to prevent quaking. Insects caused 27 percent more damage to nonquaking leaves.

KEY FACTS

The white bark has black scars.

+ leaves: Alternate, simple, to 3.2 in (8 cm); round, finely toothed, whitish beneath

+ flowers/fruits: Male and female catkins on separate trees; fruit capsule, 70–100 in catkin 4 in (10 cm) long

+ range: Alaska to Labrador, south to Mexico, Nebraska, Missouri, Virginia

In the Quaking Aspen, suckering from roots and rhizomes produces more than just a thicket; it establishes dense clonal stands. In fact, the world's heaviest (and oldest) "organism" is a clone of aspens in Utah that is 80,000 years old, weighs 13.2 million pounds (6 million kg), and covers more than 106 acres (43 ha). Named Pando (Latin for "I spread"), the stand of 43,000 male trees is in decline, possibly stressed from disease, insect damage, and drought. The aspen is remarkable visually. Its leaves have a flattened stem, which is flexible, allowing the leaves to quake in the slightest breeze. They turn brilliant yellow in fall.

Pussy Willow

Salix discolor H to 30 ft (9.1 m)

Many of us first saw the Pussy Willow not outdoors but in an arrangement of its bare spring branches with their pearl-gray male catkins, which are said to look like cats' feet.

KEY FACTS

The catkins are unstalked.

+ **leaves:** Alternate, to 4.8 in (12 cm), oval, irregularly toothed, whitish green below

+ **flowers/fruits:** Male and female catkins on different trees, dense, fuzzy; fruit capsule beaked; seeds with cottony down

+ **range:** British Columbia to Newfoundland, south into Smoky Mountains

The Pussy Willow is a small tree or a shrub with many tall stems found mostly in pure stands, and especially in wet areas. Because it tends to be shrubby, it is often planted as a hedge. There are male and female trees, and the trademark catkins are male, emerging very early in the spring; a male tree must be planted if these catkins are to be expected. They are also eaten by birds. The specific label, *discolor*, means "two-colored" (not discolored), referring to the difference in color between the green upper leaf surface and the much lighter, whitish underside.

Bebb Willow

Salix bebbiana H 15–25 ft (4.5–7.5 m)

Bebb Willows are the premier diamond willows that, probably because of a fungus, develop large, diamond-shaped depressions on the trunk—a striking motif when the wood is carved.

KEY FACTS

The bark is gray-maroon.

+ **leaves:** Alternate, to 3.5 in (9 cm), oval, white below; veins netlike; leafstalks to 0.3 in (8 mm)

+ **flowers/fruits:** Catkins unisexual, on different trees, to 3 in (7.5 cm); fruit capsule beaked, seeds with threads

+ **range:** Coast to coast in Canada and northern U.S.

The Bebb Willow is the most common willow tree in Alaska and Canada. As is common among the willows, its buds, shoots, bark, and wood provide food for many mammals. A large shrub or a small, bushy tree, it has a short trunk and a rounded crown and is found most often in moist, rich soils. It is fast growing and sprouts from the roots, creating clonal thickets, and thus is an excellent pioneer species in areas that provide the plants with sufficient moisture. It is often found with other willows. The wood is used to make baseball bats and wicker furniture.

||||||||||||||||||||||||||||||||||||||||||||||||||||||||||||||||||||||||||||||||||||||

Black Willow
Salix nigra H 30–60 ft (9–18 m)

Wood of the Black Willow is light, does not splinter readily, keeps its shape, glues well, and is easy to work. It was at one time used in the manufacture of artificial limbs, or wooden legs.

KEY FACTS

The trunk is massive.

+ leaves: Alternate, to 6 in (15 cm), narrow, finely toothed, green above and below

+ flowers/fruits: Catkins unisexual, on separate trees, to 3 in (7.6 cm), upright at branchlet ends; fruit capsule ovoid, seeds tiny and silky

+ range: Maine to Minnesota, south to Texas

The Black Willow is our largest native willow and our only commercially important one. A species of wet sites, it is largest in the lower Mississippi River region. It is fast growing and forms dense root networks and so is a good pioneer species, used to reduce erosion on stream banks. Medicinal use of willow bark dates to the time of Hippocrates (400 B.C.), when the bark was chewed to relieve inflammation. An active ingredient is salicin, a chemical compound related to aspirin (acetylsalicylic acid). Both words echo the scientific name of the family, Salicaceae, and genus, *Salix*. Other substances give willow bark antioxidant, fever-reducing, immune-boosting properties.

III

Weeping Willow
Salix babylonica H to 60 ft (18 m)

The father of taxonomy, Linnaeus, erred in naming the Weeping Willow *babylonica* for the willow of Babylon, mentioned in Psalm 137. That tree was the Euphrates poplar, *Populus euphratica.*

KEY FACTS

The twigs are flexible and greenish gold.

+ **leaves:** Alternate, to 7.1 in (18 cm), narrow, finely toothed

+ **flowers/fruits:** Catkins unisexual on separate trees, to 1 in (2.5 cm), upright; fruit capsule on catkin, to 1 in (2.5 cm)

+ **range:** Nonnative; planted widely

The graceful Weeping Willow is a native to China and one of the world's most loved trees. It was first brought to North America from Europe in 1730 for use as an ornamental. The slender, flexible branches hang vertically to the ground, in curtain-like masses. Like other willows, it grows best in moist sites and is often almost stereotypically seen growing beside a lake. Its hanging twigs are greenish gold, and its leaves turn bright yellow in the fall. It has a short trunk, with pale to dark gray, roughly ridged bark often marred with burls from which grow pale yellow shoots.

Bigleaf Maple

Acer macrophyllum H to 98 ft (30 m)

Researchers hunt for unique traits in Bigleaf Maples, hoping to amplify them in cultivars. Trees that bear red leaves—found mostly in northern California—produce triple samaras.

KEY FACTS

The leaf is the largest of any maple.

+ leaves: Opposite, to 12 in (30 cm); 5 lobes, deep, pointed; teeth few, irregular

+ flowers/fruits: Flowers unisexual, green-yellow, fragrant, on same hanging clusters; fruits paired samaras, in long clusters

+ range: Coastal, British Columbia to southern California

In the Pacific Northwest, the only maple tree that is medium size to large is the Bigleaf Maple. It grows mostly in mixed stands on moist sites but is planted for shade in cities. Its trunk is straight and its branches stout, and it is a source of commercial lumber, the wood used in musical instruments, furniture, and cabinets. Older trees produce burls that lend special beauty to veneers. Because the bark of the Bigleaf Maple holds moisture, in places like the Quinault Rain Forest in Washington's Olympic Mountains, the tree is often densely clothed in epiphytic mosses, ferns, and liverworts.

||||||||||||||||||||||||||||||||||||||||||||||||||||||||||||||||||||||||||||||||

Box Elder/Manitoba Maple
Acer negundo H to 65.6 ft (20 m)

"Box Elder" refers both to the poor-quality wood, suitable for nothing more elegant than boxes and crates, and to the supposed similarity of the leaves to those of elders *(Sambucus)*.

KEY FACTS

Fruiting is often prolific.

+ leaves: Opposite, compound, smooth; 3–9 leaflets, to 4.8 in (12 cm); teeth pointed, irregular

+ flowers/fruits: Clusters unisexual on separate trees; paired samara fruits, often in hanging clusters

+ range: Eastern United States, northwest to Alberta, to Ontario

The Box Elder, or Manitoba Maple, is our only compound-leaved maple. It is often grown ornamentally, and the cultivars include a seedless variety. It is not universally popular, however, naturalizing easily and sometimes invasive, even in North America. When it has three leaflets, it can recall Poison Ivy, but the latter has alternate leaves (the Box Elder's are opposite) and always has three leaflets (the Box Elder can have as many as nine), and its twigs are not green (the Box Elder's are). The tree is the main host of the Boxelder Bug, a black and red insect, but the bugs are more annoying than harmful.

Red Maple

Acer rubrum H to 92 ft (28 m)

The often showy Red Maple earned its specific label, *rubrum,* meaning "red." The flowers, fruit, stems, buds, and fall leaves are all red or reddish.

KEY FACTS

The samaras are red, pink, or yellow.

+ **leaves:** Opposite, pale below; 3–5 lobes, pointed, once or twice toothed

+ **flowers/fruits:** Perfect or unisexual (sometimes in unisexual clusters, on same or different trees), on slender stalk; fruits double samaras on slender stalk

+ **range:** Eastern U.S., Quebec

The Red Maple is one of the most abundant trees in eastern North America, growing on many types of soil, in many tree assemblages, and from sea level well into the Appalachian Mountains. It is often planted for shade in yards and on streets. Cultivars have been developed that are more adapted to the urban environment or that enhance red and orange foliage in the fall. The fruits are eaten by squirrels and birds, and deer and rabbits browse the shoots. The wood is used in flooring, cabinets, and furniture. Syrup is made from the sap, but it is inferior to that of the Sugar Maple.

Silver Maple

Acer saccharinum H to 98 ft (30 m)

The Silver Maple is tapped and its sap used to make syrup and sugar. For commercial success, the sugar level is too low, despite its species name, *saccharinum*, from the Latin for "sugar."

KEY FACTS

The trunk often branches low.

+ leaves: Opposite, to 7.9 in (20 cm), silvery below; 5 lobes; sinuses narrow, margin irregularly toothed

+ flowers/fruits: Unisexual clusters on same or different trees; fruits double samaras on slender stalk, prominently veined

+ range: Eastern U.S., New Brunswick

This abundant tree of wet lowlands is related to the Red Maple but lacks the red. Its leaves are intricately divided, and they seem to flicker in a breeze, their silvery undersides (thus the common name) coming in and out of view. The fruits are the largest produced by a native maple and provide food for squirrels and birds. The tree was once planted widely as an ornamental and street tree, but now people think better of it; it splits, breaks, and sheds twigs, it rots and suckers, the seeds are a nuisance, the roots can ruin pipes, and its pests excrete a sticky sap on the ground, or car, beneath.

Sugar Maple
Acer saccharum H to 98 ft (30 m)

Many maple species grow in Canada, but many Canadians consider the Sugar Maple the national tree. An iconic, five-lobed leaf of a maple is the red focus of the nation's flag.

KEY FACTS

The fall foliage is brilliant.

+ **leaves:** Opposite, to 8 in (20 cm), paler below; 3–5 lobes, pointed; teeth few, coarse

+ **flowers/fruits:** Flowers perfect or unisexual, on slim stalk to 3 in (7.5 cm), in clusters on same tree; fruits double samaras

+ **range:** Nova Scotia to southern Manitoba, south to Tennessee

The magnificent Sugar Maple is one of eastern North America's most famous trees. European colonists learned from the native peoples that the tree's sap could be collected and concentrated to make maple syrup, and concentrated some more to make sugar. In addition to its syrup, throughout its range every fall, the tree attracts thousands of people who want to see the expanse of bright color, blinding bright yellow, orange, and red—sometimes all on the same tree. A key species of the eastern hardwood forests, it is also planted in yards, on streets, and in parks. Many cultivars have been developed.

Norway Maple
Acer platanoides H to 98 ft (30 m)

The Norway Maple is one of North America's most common street tree. The popular European import has been bred for improved color, leaf shape, growth form, and urban performance.

KEY FACTS

The leaf stems exude milky sap when broken.

+ leaves: Opposite, to 6.3 in (16 cm), pointed teeth on margin; 5 lobes, mostly pointed

+ flowers/fruits: Flowers perfect or unisexual, sexes on different clusters; fruits double samaras, wings almost in a straight line

+ range: Nonnative; planted widely

Introduced to the northeast by Philadelphia botanist John Bartram in 1756, the Norway Maple is one of the most popular trees in North America, widely planted, especially in cities and towns, from Ontario to Newfoundland, from Maine to Minnesota, and south to North Carolina and Tennessee, as well as from British Columbia to Oregon, east to Idaho and Montana. Sadly, the popular nonnative has jumped its bounds to invade forests in the Northeast and the Pacific Northwest, outcompeting native species and overshading understory species. The Norway is nevertheless still widely sold in nurseries.

Ohio Buckeye/Fetid Buckeye

Aesculus glabra H 30–49 ft (9–15 m)

The seed of *Aesculus glabra* is called a buckeye, because it recalls the eye of a male deer. Carried in the pocket as a good luck charm, it was also charged with preventing rheumatism.

KEY FACTS

All parts are rank when crushed.

+ **leaves:** Opposite, compound; 5–7 leaflets, oval, pointed, to 6 in (15 cm)

+ **flowers/fruits:** Flowers perfect or unisexual, yellow, in terminal clusters to 7 in (17.8 cm); fruit a spiny capsule, to 2 in (5 cm); seeds brown, shiny, to 1.5 in (3.8 cm)

+ **range:** East-central United States

A medium-size tree, the Ohio Buckeye fares best and takes on a more pleasing form when it grows in river bottoms or on stream banks, although it grows with oaks and hickories in drier locations. Buckeye trees are not heavily used by wildlife, although squirrels will sometimes eat young buckeyes. All parts of the plant contain a toxic alkaloid that may deter would-be browsers. The Ohio Buckeye is planted often as an ornamental for its fruit and because of its bright orange fall foliage. Its light wood is used in woodcarving and was once used to manufacture artificial limbs.

Tree of Heaven/Ailanthus

Ailanthus altissima H 82 ft (25 m)

Ailanthus occurs in Ontario, Quebec, and 43 states, classed as a noxious or invasive plant in many. It should not be planted. Eliminating trees, especially females, reduces seed production.

KEY FACTS

It damages the native environment severely.

+ leaves: Alternate, compound, to 35.5 in (90 cm); 11–41 leaflets, paired along stem

+ flowers/fruits: Flowers mostly unisexual, sexes on separate trees, tiny, yellow-green, in large, conical clusters at tip of twigs; fruits double, twisted samaras in clusters

+ range: Nonnative; widely invasive

Called "tree from hell" and the "kudzu of trees," this native of China seems biologically engineered to invade. Ailanthus spreads by its profusely produced seeds and by sprouting from its roots. It produces a chemical that causes allelopathy, preventing most other plants from growing beneath it. It may be the continent's fastest growing tree, adding 3 to 6 feet (1–2 m) a year when young. What's more, its value to wildlife is virtually nil, and its wood is useless. First brought to North America in 1784, it was planted extensively as a street tree in the 1800s, faring well under the stresses of city life. But the opportunist soon turns a clearing into a dense, impenetrable mass of stems.

American Basswood

Tilia americana H 65–82 ft (20–25 m)

The American Basswood has been widely used medicinally—for example, to treat headache or digestive ailments. It is now said that overconsumption can cause heart problems.

KEY FACTS

The flower stalk has a long, leafy bract.

+ **leaves:** Alternate, to 8 in (20 cm), toothed; base unequally heart-shaped

+ **flowers/fruits:** Flowers perfect, to 0.6 in (1.5 cm), creamy, fragrant, 5 petals, few on stalk; fruit a nutlet, to 0.4 in (1.2 cm) across

+ **range:** Central, eastern U.S.; southern Ontario, Quebec

This stately tree of the lowland woods is the best known of our native basswoods, although the European species (lindens) are better suited for life in cities. The American Basswood has a straight trunk, unbranched for half its length, and a broad crown. Found mostly in mixed stands in rich soils, it is important to wildlife: It naturally develops cavities that attract cavity nesters like woodpeckers and Wood Ducks, and squirrels and quail eat its seeds. The timber is important in the Great Lakes region, used in cabinetry, musical instruments, boxes, excelsior, and pulp. Native peoples made thread and cord from its tough inner bark.

Common Hackberry

Celtis occidentalis H 32–60 ft (10–18 m)

Detracting from the Common Hackberry's beauty are "witches' brooms," abnormal but harmless tufts of short twigs often formed in its branches, probably caused by a fungus and a mite.

KEY FACTS

The bark has corky ridges.

+ **leaves:** Alternate, to 3.5 in (8.9 cm), toothed near pointed tip, base unevenly rounded

+ **flowers/fruits:** Flowers perfect or unisexual, on same plant; fruit a drupe, to 0.8 in (2 cm), orange turning purple

+ **range:** Southern Ontario and Quebec; midwestern, northeastern U.S.

The small to medium-size Common Hackberry excels in moist, fertile places but is drought tolerant and thrives in sandy soils, too. It has a straight trunk with thick branches. Its common name refers to the fruit and derives from "hagberry," a British word for a tree similar to the Chokecherry. The fruit is edible and sweet, though usually out of reach. The fruits are somewhat important to wildlife, including raccoons, squirrels, and game birds. The weak, soft wood is nonetheless used in some furniture and in fences, posts, and boxes. The Hackberry is planted in gardens and as a street tree.

American Elm
Ulmus americana H 132 ft (40 m)

American Elms lined many streets, especially in northeastern states, but Dutch Elm disease, a fungus carried by Elm Bark Beetles, has ravaged the trees. All elm species are susceptible.

KEY FACTS

The tree is vase-shaped.

+ **leaves:** Alternate, to 6 in (15 cm), rough above, toothed, pointed, uneven at base

+ **flowers/fruits:** Flowers perfect, small, 3–5 on slim, drooping stalk; fruits flat sama-ras, to 0.5 in (1.3 cm), deeply notched at tip; seeds with papery wing

+ **range:** East; southern Canada south

Many native peoples selected a towering American Elm as the site for councils and other important events, and the stately, graceful tree held Europeans similarly in awe. In many other ways, this is among the most important trees of eastern North America. In the wild, it tolerates a range of soils, usually growing alongside other hardwoods. Its buds, flowers, and fruits feed mammals and birds, and its twigs provide forage for larger mammals. Some cultivars have been developed that show some resistance to Dutch Elm disease. It is hoped that the same can be done for another deadly threat facing elms—elm yellows (see p. 163).

Slippery Elm

Ulmus rubra H 49–82 ft (15–25 m)

This tree is named for its mucilaginous inner bark. The bark, a cough remedy before European contact, stayed in the U.S. Pharmacopeia until 1960 and is still used in cough preparations.

KEY FACTS

The trunk branches high in the tree.

+ leaves: Alternate, to 6.3 in (16 cm), dark green, hairy below

+ flowers/fruits: Flowers perfect, small, few, in crowded clusters on short stalk; fruit a samara, to 0.5 in (1.3 cm) across, slightly notched at tip, hairy

+ range: Southern Ontario through most of eastern U.S.

This lowland tree usually grows with other hardwoods. Its seeds are not of great importance to wildlife, but it provides some browse for deer and rabbits. The scientific name means "red elm," another of its common names, reflecting the red-brown wood. It is used for boxes, crates, and baskets. Native peoples used its bark for canoe shells when birch was not available. The Slippery Elm (and the American) is threatened by elm yellows, a disease spread by leafhoppers that attacks the trees' transport tissues. The first symptoms are yellowing, drooping, or early loss of leaves, but by the time they appear, it is too late.

||||||||||||||||||||||||||||||||||||||||||||||||||||||||||||||||||||||||||||||||

Rock Elm

Ulmus thomasii H 82–115 ft (25–35 m)

Even though the Rock Elm's claim to fame is its hard wood, it is often called Cork Elm because its older branches can bear three or four thick, irregular corky wings.

KEY FACTS

The fruits are a key trait.

+ leaves: Alternate, to 4 in (10 cm), coarsely toothed, on hairy stalk

+ flowers/fruits: Flowers perfect, small, reddish, 2–4 in dangling clusters; fruit samara, flat, broad winged, slightly notched at tip

+ range: Northern U.S. Midwest, east to northeastern U.S., southern Canada

The Rock Elm is not a tree of pure stands but is usually found growing alongside such species as American Elm, Basswood, Sugar Maple, and White Ash. While it prefers a moist, well-drained loam, it also grows on drier, upland sites, including those on limestone. Some argue that growth on a rocky substrate earned it its common name, but most say it refers to the wood. The heaviest, hardest elm wood, it has few knots, bends well, and can take shock. That makes it superior when strength is mandatory, so it has seen use in ships' timbers, curved sections of furniture, early refrigerators and car bodies, hockey sticks, and ax handles.

Creosote Bush

Larrea tridentata H 3.3–10 ft (1–3 m)

Native peoples used the fragrant Creosote Bush for many medical purposes. The resin also served as a glue for mending broken pottery or cementing a projectile point to its shaft.

KEY FACTS

Nodes make the stem look jointed.

+ leaves: Evergreen, opposite, compound; 2 leaflets, to 0.7 in (1.8 cm), resinous, joined basally

+ flowers/fruits: Flowers to 1 in (2.5 cm) across, velvety, axillary; 5 yellow petals; capsule 5-parted, fuzzy

+ range: Southern California, east to Utah and Texas

The Creosote Bush is a trademark of the Mojave Desert. In full bloom, the flowers lend the plant a yellowish cast, and after a rain, the resin exudes a tarry aroma. Its main value to wildlife is as shelter. Kangaroo Rats and Desert Tortoises are two animals that bed down under the plant. The Creosote Bush Grasshopper eats this plant exclusively, having evolved digestive processes allowing it to process the mostly inedible resin. A Creosote Bush can live 100 years, but when it dies, stems sprout at its edge, creating a Creosote Bush ring. One ring, called King Clone, has been aged with radiocarbon dating at 11,700 years. Its diameter averages 45 feet (13.7 m).

Joshua Tree

Yucca brevifolia H to 50 ft (15 m)

Other members of the genus *Yucca* are probably more familiar to the reader, and it helps to recall their leaves (living and dead) and flowers when contemplating the Joshua Tree.

KEY FACTS

Plants can sprout from rhizomes.

+ **leaves:** Evergreen, to 9 in (23 cm), spear-like, sharply toothed, in rosettes at branch ends

+ **flowers/fruits:** Flowers perfect, white, clustered at branch tips; 6 tepals; fruits to 5 in (13 cm), 3-angled, light red to yellow-brown

+ **range:** Endemic to Mojave Desert

The striking Joshua Tree seems to branch wildly, but closer examination reveals that each branching results in two equivalent, stout branches more or less at a right angle to each other. The branches are armed with horrific spines and are tipped with clusters of bladelike leaves that recall a Common Yucca plant. The tree remains unbranched, though, until it blooms the first time (or until its tip is somehow damaged). Old leaves persist, folded back and shaggy along the branches, which bear a thick, furrowed bark. In a sort of give-and-take, Yucca Moths pollinate the flowers, which open at night, and lay their eggs inside them, where eventually their larvae will undergo metamorphosis.

Cuban Royal Palm/Florida Royal Palm

Roystonea regia H to 131 ft (40 m)

Palms are indispensable to people who need to use them for food, fiber, sugar, wax, and wood. Palms are commercially important, too, as the source of rattan, oils, coconuts, and acai.

KEY FACTS

The crownshaft is conspicuous.

+ leaves: To 13 ft (4 m), compound, featherlike; many strap-shaped leaflets

+ flowers/fruits: Flowers unisexual, on same tree, to 0.3 in (8 mm) across, white, fragrant, in hanging clusters to 2 ft (0.6 m); drupes, to 0.6 in (1.5 cm), black

+ range: Southern Florida

In addition to its long, feathery leaves, the Cuban Royal Palm is distinguished from others by the occasional bulge along its trunk and, just below its canopy, by the bright glossy green "crownshaft." The crownshaft is made up of the bases of the leaves, the older ones closer to the outside. When a leaf has died, its base will eventually separate from the tree, leaving a new ringed scar just below the crownshaft on the light gray trunk. The tree is a tall, unbranched column with a spreading crown of leaves. The flowers are pollinated by bees and bats, and bats, as well as birds, eat the fruit and disperse the seeds.

III

Cabbage Palmetto

Sabal palmetto H to 82 ft (25 m)

This palmetto is named for its terminal bud, or heart of palm, where new fronds originate. "Swamp Cabbage" may be eaten raw or cooked. Once the bud is taken, the tree stops growing.

KEY FACTS

The trunk is straight and unbranched.

+ leaves: Leafstalk to 7.5 ft (2.3 m), serving as midrib; blade fan-like, to 6.6 ft (2 m)

+ flowers/fruits: Flowers perfect, small, white, in clusters to 6.6 ft (2 m); drupes, to 0.5 in (1.2 cm), black

+ range: Florida Keys, in Coastal Plain into North Carolina

The Cabbage Palmetto is a tree of the marshes, woodlands, and sandy soils of the Coastal Plain and is tolerant of salt spray. It is a straight, slender tree that is often grown in yards and along streets. This plant does not have a crownshaft; its leaves are produced by a terminal meristem. Native peoples harvested the fibers from the leafstalks and used them for scrubbing and to make straps and baskets. The fibers were not just used locally, though. They have been found among artifacts from the Winnebago in Wisconsin and the Iroquois of New York, as far as 700 miles (1,100 km) north of the Cabbage Palmetto's northern limit.

Saw Palmetto

Serenoa repens H to 23 ft (7 m)

Extracts of Saw Palmetto fruit are the top herbal treatment for benign prostatic hyperplasia, and research has shown that the extract can indeed improve urinary symptoms and flow volume.

KEY FACTS

The "saw" is the spiny leafstalk.

+ leaves: Leafstalk to 5 ft (1.5 m), ending in fanlike blade to 3.3 ft (1 m)

+ flowers/fruits: Flowers perfect, small, white, in clusters to 3.3 ft (1 m); drupes, to 0.8 in (2 cm), blue-black

+ range: South Carolina to southern Florida, west to Louisiana

The Saw Palmetto is not an erect palm. Instead, it sprawls along the ground, with fronds growing at the ends of long, branching, horizontal stems running as far as 15 feet (4.6 m) at or just below ground level. The result is a dense understory in pine flatwoods and scrub habitats. Some species associated with Saw Palmetto are the Crested Caracara, Sand Skink, Florida Mouse, and endangered Florida Scrub Jay. When the fruits are ripe, black bears will wander from their home range to eat them. Honey made from Saw Palmetto flowers is of high quality and commercial value.

Key Thatch Palm/<small>Brittle Thatch Palm</small>

Leucothrinax morrisii H to 40 ft (12 m)

The Key Thatch Palm, long called *Thrinax morrisii,* was given its own genus, *Leucothrinax,* after taxonomists found that it differed genetically from other *Thrinax* species.

KEY FACTS

The fronds are green and silver.

+ leaves: Leafstalk to 3.3 ft (1 m), smooth; blade fan-shaped, to 32 in (80 cm)

+ flowers/fruits: Flowers perfect, ivory-white, fragrant, tubular, in elongate, branching cluster to 6.6 ft (2 m); drupes, to 0.3 in (7 mm), white

+ range: Southern Florida

The slow-growing Key Thatch Palm has a slender, columnar trunk, with smooth, gray to brownish bark. Capped with a rounded, open crown of magnificent green and silver fronds, it is often planted as a specimen tree in the landscape or in small groups. As in other species, when grown in full sun, it will develop a denser, rounder crown, and in shadier conditions, the canopy is much more open. In nature, this tree is found in a range of habitats including the seashore and pineland sand. The Key Thatch Palm's leaves have long been used to make brooms and mats, though today these are more for decoration than for utilitarian purposes.

California Washingtonia/California Fan Palm

Washingtonia filifera H to 50 ft (15 m)

The iconic palms of Los Angeles were planted for the 1932 Summer Olympics. They will be replaced someday with native broadleafs. The palms are nonnative Mexican Washingtonias.

KEY FACTS

The leaflet edges bear threads.

+ **leaves:** Leafstalk to 5 ft (1.5 m), with hooked spines, bearing fan to 5 ft (1.5 m)

+ **flowers/fruits:** Flowers perfect, small, white, fragrant, in clusters to 16.5 ft (5 m); drupes, to 0.4 in (9 mm), almost black

+ **range:** Southwestern Arizona and southeastern California

The California Washingtonia is a columnar palm that is well known but rare, restricted in nature to streams and canyons that offer more water than the adjacent desert. It is planted in tropical areas around the world, especially along city boulevards like those in South Florida. As beautiful as the California species is, the Mexican Washingtonia *(W. robusta)* is prettier and faster growing. Other traits that make it stand out are its slimmer trunk, its height (to 75 feet/23 m vs. 50 feet/15 m in the California), its bright green leaves (vs. gray-green), and its less thready leaflet edges (*filifera* is Latin for "making threads" or "thread-bearing").

Natural Regions of North America

The continental United States and Canada can be divided into nine physiographic regions.

Appalachian Highlands

The oldest mountain chain in North America, the heavily eroded Appalachians extend for about 2,000 miles (3,200 km) from Alabama to Newfoundland, with the highest peak being Mount Mitchell, in North Carolina, at 6,684 feet (2,040 m). This mountain range started forming 480 million years ago, when continental collisions caused volcanic activity and mountain building. Ecologically, this region hosts eastern temperate forests with a great variety of coniferous and deciduous trees and wildflowers, some of them high-elevation specialists.

Coastal Plain

This gradually rising flatland spans some 4,000 miles (6,400 km) in total and covers several distantly related regions along the Gulf of Mexico, the southern Atlantic coast, and the northernmost coasts of the Arctic Ocean. In the past, oceans covered these plains, depositing sediment layers over millions of years, until falling sea levels exposed them. The types of vegetation in these widely separated regions range from subtropical trees and flowers in the southernmost coastal plain to marsh plants along the mid-Atlantic to the largely treeless tundra on the northern coast of Alaska.

Interior Plains

Ranging from the lowlands of the St. Lawrence River Valley in the east to the mile-high Great Plains in the west, the vast Interior Plains of North America provide fertile soils, especially for productive prairie farms. A shallow sea covered much of this region as recently as 75 million years ago, and sediments from rivers draining the Appalachians and western mountains were deposited in layers throughout the sea. The Great Plains were once covered by vast and diverse expanses of natural grasses, sagebrush, and a varied suite of wildflowers. Much of this ecosystem has vanished, the land brought into use by modern agriculture and extensive grazing.

Interior Highlands

The Ozark Plateau and Ouachita Mountains form the Interior Highlands, which are centered on Arkansas and southern Missouri, with mountains reaching more than 2,600 feet (800 m) high. These ancient eroded highlands were connected to the Appalachians until tectonic activity separated them some 200 million years ago. Ecologically, this relatively small area straddles the southern Interior Plains and the eastern Coastal Plain, with trees and wildflowers representing both regions.

Rocky Mountains

The highest mountain system in North America, the Rockies domi-
nate the landscape for some 3,000 miles (4,800 km), from New
Mexico to Alaska, with more than 50 peaks surpassing 14,000 feet
(4,300 m). Tectonic activity uplifted the Rockies about 50 to 100
million years ago, making them much younger and less eroded
than the Appalachians. The ecological hallmarks of the Rockies are
its coniferous forests of pines, firs, and spruces, adapted to high
elevations, with wildflower species similarly adapted to elevations
and temperatures.

Intermontane Basins and Plateaus

This region is called intermontane because it is situated between
the Pacific and the Rocky Mountain systems. Pacific mountains
block most moisture-bearing clouds coming from the Pacific
Ocean, giving desert climates to places like the Colorado Plateau,
5,000 to 7,000 feet (1,500 to 2,100 m) high, and the Great Basin.
In Canada and Alaska, the immense Yukon River Valley and the
Yukon-Tanana Uplands are part of this region. The deserts feature
cacti and a host of other specialist plants of the arid West. Cottonwoods, ashes, and willows line rivers that run intermittently through
the dry plains.

Pacific Mountain System

From Alaska to California, mountains and volcanoes tower over the
west coast in an almost unbroken chain. These mountain ranges are
geologically young and seismically active, with uplift starting some
five million years ago. The highest mountain in North America, Alaska's Mount McKinley (20,320 feet/6,200 m), is still growing at about a
millimeter a year—about the thickness of a fingernail. Distantly separated from the Rockies, this mountain range supports its own distinct
varieties of trees and wildflowers adapted to higher elevations.

Canadian Shield

The geologic core of North America is the Canadian Shield, which
contains the continent's oldest rocks. Landforms are relatively flat,

having been eroded and scoured by glaciers over millions of years. The exposed bedrock ranges in age from 570 million to more than 3 billion years old. This is a vast and extensively diverse region of climatic extremes and varied vegetation, from dense boreal forests in the south to frigid tundra in the north, populated by stunted trees, small shrubs, lichens, and ground-clinging herbs.

Arctic Lands

Highlands known as the Innuitian Mountains cover most islands. The icy climate is too harsh for most animals and vegetation, and much of the ground is permanently frozen. Nevertheless, low-growing shrubs, small tundra plants, and lichens manage to survive.

About the Author

BLAND CROWDER served as associate director and editor with the Flora of Virginia Project, whose *Flora of Virginia* was published in print and electronic formats in December 2012. A freelance writer and editor, he lives in Richmond, Virginia.

About the Artist

JARED TRAVNICEK is a medical illustrator with an M.A. in medical and biological illustration from the Johns Hopkins University School of Medicine. He is based in Indianapolis, Indiana, where he works as a neurosurgical illustrator.

Further Resources

BOOKS

Dirr, Michael A. *Manual of Woody Landscape Plants: Their Identification, Ornamental Characteristics, Culture, Propagation and Uses,* 4th ed. Stipes Publishing Co., 1990.

Elias, Thomas S. *The Complete Trees of North America: A Field Guide and Natural History.* Gramercy Publishing Co., 1987.

Harris, James G., and Melinda Woolf Harris. *Plant Identification Terminology: An Illustrated Glossary.* Spring Lake Publishing, 2001.

Rushforth, Keith, and Charles Hollis. *National Geographic Society Field Guide to Trees of North America.* National Geographic Society, 2006.

Rutkow, Eric. *American Canopy: Trees, Forests, and the Making of a Nation.* Scribner, 2012.

Sibley, David Allen. *The Sibley Guide to Trees.* Alfred A. Knopf, 2009.

WEBSITES

Flora of North America
www.efloras.org

Lady Bird Johnson Wildflower Center
www.wildflower.org

Missouri Botanical Garden Plant Finder
www.missouribotanicalgarden.org/gardens
-gardening/your-garden/plant-finder.aspx

University of Connecticut Plant Database
hort.uconn.edu

USDA Forest Service Fire Effects Information System
www.feis-crs.org

Virginia Tech Dendrology Factsheets
www.dendro.cnre.vt.edu/dendrology/factsheets.cfm

Illustrations Credits

All artwork appearing in this book was created by Jared Travnicek.

Front Cover
UP: David Noton/naturepl.com; LO (left to right): B Christopher/Alamy; David Cavagnaro/ Visuals Unlimited, Inc.; Jurgen & Christine Sohns/Minden Pictures; B. Speckart/Shutterstock.

Spine
Larry Michael/Minden Pictures.

Back Cover
LO: (left to right): Nigel Bean/Minden Pictures; Darlyne A. Murawski/National Geographic Creative; Kazuma Anezaki/Nature Production/Minden Pictures; De Agostini/Getty Images.

2-3, Darlyne A. Murawski/National Geographic Creative; 4, Floris van Breugel/NPL/ Minden Pictures; 7, Raymond Gehman/National Geographic Creative; 9, Tim Fitzharris/ Minden Pictures; 13, Photos Lamontagne/Getty Images; 14, Barrett & MacKay/All Canada Photos/Getty Images; 15, Richard Thom/Visuals Unlimited/Getty Images; 16, Ted Kinsman/Science Source; 17, Terry Donnelly; 18, Tim Fitzharris/Minden Pictures; 19, Tony Wood/Science Source; 20, Perry Mastrovito/First Light/Corbis; 21, Ron & Diane Salmon/ Flying Fish Photography LLC; 22, Ron Hutchinson Photography; 23, David Hosking/Alamy; 24, Bob Gibbons/Science Source; 25, David Matherly/Visuals Unlimited/Getty Images; 26, John Hagstrom; 27, Stephen J. Krasemann/Science Source; 28, Philippe Clement/NPL/ Minden Pictures; 29, Michael P. Gadomski/Science Source; 30, Susan Glascock; 31, Fred Bruemmer/Getty Images; 32, Michael P. Gadomski/Science Source; 33, David Hosking/ FLPA/Minden Pictures; 34, Ted Kinsman/Science Source; 35, Visuals Unlimited, Inc./Rob Kurtzman/Getty Images; 36, David Hosking/Minden Pictures; 37, Bob Gibbons/Science Source; 38, Kenneth W Fink/Getty Images; 39, Bob Gibbons/Minden Pictures; 40, Inga Spence/Science Source; 41, Thomas & Pat Leeson/Science Source; 42 & 43, Gerald D. Tang; 44, Susan Glascock; 45, Dennis Flaherty/Getty Images; 46, Michael P. Gadomski/ Science Source; 47, Keith Rushforth/Minden Pictures; 48, David Middleton/NHPA/ Photoshot; 49, David Jensen; 50, Cora Niele/Getty Images; 51, Jim Zipp/Science Source; 52, David Winkelman/David Liebman; 53, Ron & Diane Salmon/Flying Fish Photography LLC; 54, Susan Glascock; 55, David Jensen; 56, Ethan Welty/Aurora Photos; 57, Ron & Diane Salmon/Flying Fish Photography LLC; 58, Tim Fitzharris/Minden Pictures; 59, Ron & Diane Salmon/Flying Fish Photography LLC; 60, David Woodfall/Photoshot Holdings Ltd/Alamy; 61, Michael P. Gadomski/Science Source; 62 & 63, Ron & Diane Salmon/Flying Fish Photography LLC; 64, Carr Clifton/Minden Pictures; 65, Colin Marshall/FLPA/Minden Pictures; 66, Ron & Diane Salmon/Flying Fish Photography LLC; 67, Jim Brandenburg/ Minden Pictures; 68, Inga Spence/Science Source; 69, David Liebman; 70, Kenneth Murray/Science Source; 71, Adam Jones/Science Source; 72, James Steakley; 73, Inga Spence/Science Source; 74, Geoff Bryant/Science Source; 75, Frank Zullo/Science Source; 76, Adam Jones/Science Source; 77, Ron Boardman/Life Science Image/FLPA/Science Source; 78, Gerald D. Tang; 79, Dave Watts/Alamy; 80, Tim Fitzharris/Minden Pictures/ Getty Images; 81, Geoff Kidd/Science Source; 82, William Weber/Visuals Unlimited, Inc.; 83, Joel Sartore/National Geographic/Getty Images; 84, Ron & Diane Salmon/Flying Fish Photography LLC; 85, Panoramic Images/Getty Images; 86, DEA/C.SAPPA/De Agostini/ Getty Images; 87, Dane Johnson/Visuals Unlimited, Inc.; 88, Michael Orton/Getty Images; 89, Doug Sokell/Visuals Unlimited, Inc.; 90, John Shaw/Science Source; 91, Gerald D. Tang; 92, Mark Oatney/Getty Images; 93, Eliot Cohen; 94, Kent Foster/Science Source; 95, Phillip Merritt; 96, Marcos Issa/Argosfoto; 97, John Glover/Alamy; 98, De Agostini/S. Montanari/ Getty Images; 99, Peter Chadwick LRPS/Getty Images; 100, Melinda Fawver/Shutterstock; 101, E. R. Degginger/Science Source; 102, Lee F. Snyder/Science Source; 103, Stuart Wilson/Science Source; 104, Altrendo Nature/Getty Images; 105, Ron & Diane Salmon/ Flying Fish Photography LLC; 106, Adam Jones/Science Source; 107, Michael P. Gadomski/ Science Source; 108, Stan Osolinski/Oxford Scientific/Getty Images; 109, William Webber/

ILLUSTRATIONS CREDITS
||||||||||||||||||||||||||||||||||||||||||||||||||||||||||||||||||||||||||||||||||||||||||||||||||||||||||||

Visuals Unlimited, Inc.; 110, shapencolour/Alamy; 111, Ron & Diane Salmon/Flying Fish Photography LLC; 112, Anne Gilbert/Alamy; 113, Ron & Diane Salmon/Flying Fish Photography LLC; 114, Susan A Roth/Alamy; 115, Mack Henley/Visuals Unlimited, Inc.; 116-120, Ron & Diane Salmon/Flying Fish Photography LLC; 121, DEA/S. MONTANARI/Getty Images; 122, Gerald D. Tang; 123, Ron & Diane Salmon/Flying Fish Photography LLC; 124, Br. Alfred Brousseau, Saint Mary's College; 125, Ron & Diane Salmon/Flying Fish Photography LLC; 126, A. N. T./Science Source; 127, Charles Bush/Alamy; 128, Dorling Kindersley/Getty Images; 129, Jodie Coston/Getty Images; 130, James Young/Getty Images; 131, Ron & Diane Salmon/Flying Fish Photography LLC; 132, Eliot Cohen; 133, Plantography/Alamy; 134, David Winkelman/David Liebman; 135, Karl Magnacca; 136, M Timothy O'Keefe/Getty Images; 137, Laura Berman/Green Fuse Photos; 138, Alex Hare/Getty Images; 139, Richard Shiell; 140, Q-Images/Alamy; 141, Eliot Cohen; 142, Ed Jensen; 143, Michael P. Gadomski/Science Source; 144, Gerald & Buff Corsi/Visuals Unlimited, Inc.; 145, Doug Sokell/Visuals Unlimited, Inc.; 146, Joseph Sohm/Visions of America/Corbis; 147, James Steinberg/Science Source; 148, Dwight Kuhn; 149, Eliot Cohen; 150, Michael P Gadomski/Getty Images; 151, David Roth/Botanica/Getty Images; 152, Gary Vestal/Getty Images; 153, DEA/RANDOM/Getty Images; 154-156, Ron & Diane Salmon/Flying Fish Photography LLC; 157, Geoff Kidd/Science Source; 158, Gilbert Twiest/Visuals Unlimited, Inc.; 159, Martin Page/Getty Images; 160, Kathleen Nelson/Alamy; 161, Jim Brandenburg/Minden Pictures/Getty Images; 162, Ron & Diane Salmon/Flying Fish Photography LLC; 163 & 164, John Hagstrom; 165, Nature's Images/Science Source; 166, Carr Clifton/Minden Pictures; 167, Susan Webb/Flying Fish Photography LLC; 168, Nature's Images, Inc./Science Source; 169, Kenneth Murray/Science Source; 170, Kyle Wicomb; 171, Eliot Cohen; 175, Lark Garges Smith.

Index

Boldface indicates species profile.

A

Abies
  amabilis **20**
  balsamea **21**
  fraseri **22**
  grandis **23**
  lasiocarpa **29**
  magnifica **24**
Acer
  macrophyllum **152**
  negundo **153**
  platanoides **157**
  pseudoplatanus 132
  rubrum **154**
  saccharinum **155**
  saccharum **156**
Aesculus glabra **158**
Ailanthus (Ailanthus altissima) **159**
Alaska Cedar **13**
Albizia julibrissin **74**
Alder
  Hazel **57**
  Red **56**
Alnus
  rubra **56**
  serrulata **57**
Amelanchier
  alnifolia **137**
  arborea **74**
Aralia spinosa **54**
Arborvitae **19**
Artemisia tridentata **55**
Ash
  Green **130**
  White **129**, 130, 164
Asimina triloba **50**
Atlantic White Cedar **14**

B

Baldcypress 8, 14, **18**, 93, 127
Basswood, American **160**
Bayberry
  Pacific **124**
  Southern **125**
Beech, American **83**
Betula
  alleghaniensis **58**
  lenta 62
  nigra **59**
  occidentalis **60**
  papyrifera **61**
  uber **62**
Birch
  Paper/White 21, **61**
  River **59**
  Sweet 62
  Virginia Roundleaf/
    Ashe's **62**
  Water **60**
  Yellow **58**
Black Walnut **106**
Blackgum/Black Tupelo
  14, **128**
Blueberries 72, **73**, 137
Bluegum, Tasmanian **126**
Box Elder **153**
Buckeye, Ohio/Fetid
  158
Buckthorn, California
  135
Buttonwood **132**

C

Cactus
  Jumping Cholla 8, **65**
  Saguaro **64**, 75
California Laurel **115**
Carnegiea gigantea **64**
Carya
  cordiformis **107**
  glabra **108**
  illinoinensis **109**
  laciniosa **110**
  ovata **111**
  tomentosa **112**
Castanea dentata **82**
Catalpa
  bignonioides **63**
  speciosa 63
Celtis occidentalis **161**
Cenchrus ciliaris 75

Cercis canadensis 74, **76**
Chamaecyparis
  nootkatensis **13**
  thyoides **14**
Cherry
  Black Cherry 95, **141**
  Chokecherry **143**, 161
Chestnut, American 70, 82
Chinaberry Tree **120**
Cholla, Jumping 8, **65**
Coach Whip. *see* Ocotillo
Coffeeberry, California.
  see Buckthorn,
  California
Cornus
  drummondii **66**
  florida **67**
  nuttallii **68**
Cottonwood
  Black **144**
  Eastern **145**
  Plains **146**
Cranberry 73
Crataegus species **138**
Creosote Bush **165**
Cucumber-tree **117**
Cupressus 13
Cylindropuntia fulgida **65**
Cypresses, false
  Alaska Cedar **13**
  Atlantic White Cedar **14**
Cypresses, true 13; *see also* Baldcypress

D

Devil's Walkingstick **54**
Diospyros virginiana **69**
Dogwood
  Flowering **67**, 68
  Pacific **68**
  Roughleaf **66**
Douglas-fir 23, 28, **46**, 90

E

Elders 153
Elm
  American **162**, 163, 164
  Rock **164**
  Slippery **163**

National Geographic
Pocket Guide to the Trees & Shrubs
of North America

Published by the National Geographic Society

Gary E. Knell, *President and Chief Executive Officer*

John M. Fahey, *Chairman of the Board*

Declan Moore, *Chief Media Officer*

Chris Johns, *Chief Content Officer*

Prepared by the Book Division

Hector Sierra, *Senior Vice President and General Manager*

Janet Goldstein, *Senior Vice President and Editorial Director*

Jonathan Halling, *Creative Director*

Marianne R. Koszorus, *Design Director*

Susan Tyler Hitchcock, *Senior Editor*

R. Gary Colbert, *Production Director*

Jennifer A. Thornton, *Director of Managing Editorial*

Susan S. Blair, *Director of Photography*

Meredith C. Wilcox, *Director, Administration and Rights Clearance*

Staff for This Book

Barbara Payne, *Editor*

Paul Hess, *Text Editor*

Andrea Wollitz, *Project Editor*

Sanáa Akkach, *Art Director*

Linda Makarov, *Designer*

Katie Olsen, *Production Design Manager*

Noelle Weber, *Production Designer*

Catherine Herbert Howell, *Developmental Editor*

Miriam Stein, *Illustrations Editor*

Carl Mehler, *Director of Maps*

Uliana Bazar, *Art Researcher*

Marshall Kiker, *Associate Managing Editor*

Judith Klein, *Production Editor*

Galen Young, *Rights Clearance Specialist*

Rachel Faulise, *Manager, Production Services*

The National Geographic Society is one of the world's largest nonprofit scientific and educational organizations. Its mission is to inspire people to care about the planet. Founded in 1888, the Society is member supported and offers a community for members to get closer to explorers, connect with other members, and help make a difference. The Society reaches more than 450 million people worldwide each month through *National Geographic* and other magazines; National Geographic Channel; television documentaries; music; radio; films; books; DVDs; maps; exhibitions; live events; school publishing programs; interactive media; and merchandise. National Geographic has funded more than 10,000 scientific research, conservation, and exploration projects and supports an education program promoting geographic literacy. For more information, visit www.nationalgeographic.com.

For more information, please call 1-800-NGS LINE (647-5463) or write to the following address:

National Geographic Society
1145 17th Street N.W.
Washington, D.C. 20036-4688 U.S.A.

For information about special discounts for bulk purchases, please contact National Geographic Books Special Sales: ngspecsales@ngs.org

For rights or permissions inquiries, please contact National Geographic Books Subsidiary Rights: ngbookrights@ngs.org

ISBN: 978-1-4262-1475-2

Printed in Hong Kong

14/THK/1

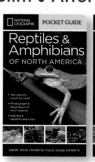
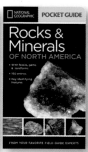
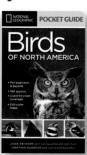